ISLAM AND THE VEDAS

The Koran and Vedic literatures Reconciled

Rāsamaṇḍala dās

Interfaith Dialogue

ISLAM AND THE VEDAS

The Koran and Vedic literatures Reconciled

authorHOUSE®

Rāsamaṇḍala dās

Interfaith Dialogue

AuthorHouse™
1663 Liberty Drive
Bloomington, IN 47403
www.authorhouse.com
Phone: 1-800-839-8640

Published by AuthorHouse 04/24/2012

ISBN: 978-1-4567-9748-5 (sc)
ISBN: 978-1-4567-9750-8 (e)

Dedication

To *Lokanātha Swami* whose patience, tolerance, and gentle behavior touched my heart.

To *Śrīla A.C. Bhaktivedanta Swami Prabhupāda* who is so kind to me.

To his earnest admirers who encouraged me in so many ways.

Acknowledgment

I am very grateful to *Akhilādhārā Prabhu* for working with me as editor in the production of this book. His steady enthusiasm, encouragement and commitment helped shape this book to give it its present form. I am very thankful to *Dāmodara Paṇḍit Prabhu* who went through the whole manuscript once again. I am much indebted to *Lokanātha Swami* who inspired me to undertake this humble effort to unite those who seek the ultimate peace, harmony and truth, which lies only in understanding the essence of the Lord's message.

Appreciations

A comparative study between Vedic literature and the Koran is a helpful step towards cross-cultural appreciation. This study is not only meant to deepen one's own tradition but also hopes to promote harmony, unity and peace between individuals in the world. A basic knowledge of both traditions is awaiting the reader who will be surprised to discover that the Vedic tradition very much parallels the Islamic teachings. Within this book both scriptures are carefully examined with sobriety and scholarship. I truly hope that this study will help those sincere souls who are in search of the absolute truth.

Lokanātha Swami
Director Bhaktivedanta Academy for Spiritual Science, India
Author of Kumbha, Festivals, Sanskrit Pronunciation

Some Muslim sages of old referred to Brahmins as followers of Abraham and to the Vedas as the primordial revelation of monotheism. This important work in a sense pursues the consequences of the symbolic meaning of this dictum and creates a Vaishnavite interpretation of the Koran in relation to the Vedas, demonstrating deep affinities between the first and last revealed scriptures of present day humanity. May this book help to bring closer together the followers of Islam and Hinduism especially in India where there is such a profound need for greater accord between the followers of these two major religions.

Seyyed Hossein Nasr
Professor of Islamic Studies at George Washington University
Prominent Islamic Philosopher
Renowned scholar of comparative religion
Author of more than fifty scholarly books and articles

"This remarkable inter-textual reading of Islamic scripture from a Vaishnava perspective is a thought-provoking contribution to interreligious relations."

Carl W. Ernst, William R. Kenan, Jr.
Distinguished Professor of Religious Studies,
The University of North Carolina at Chapel Hill NC
Author of Following Muhammad, Rethinking Islam in the Contemporary World

This comparative study takes a step towards reconciliation between two of the world's great religious scriptures, the Koran and Vedic literature. Rāsamaṇḍala dās ingeniously cites verses with the same teachings from both scriptures. Thus he provides a middle ground for brotherhood and acceptance under the worship of God: One small step for mankind and a giant step for spiritual harmony.

Dean. C. Neeskens (B.ED., M.ED) University of Sydney
President Association for Vedic arts and Culture, Australia

This comparative study between the Koran and Vedic literature is a welcomed contribution. It is a call for the urgent need to appreciate the common and fundamental spiritual values between Islam and Hinduism. My post graduate studies of comparing the ancient traditional Vedic educational systems and the Indonesian system convinced me of the close harmony and unity between the Islamic faith and the Vedic culture. In a world racing towards better socio-cultural exchanges, this vital message presented by Rāsamaṇḍala dās is timely, essential and imperative for all scholars, scientists, leaders, students and believers of all faiths. It is a clarion call for interreligious solidarity and unity.

Real L.J. Gagnon (Bhakti Raghava Swami) B.A, M. Ed
University of Ottawa, Canada / State University of Yogyakarta, Indonesia
Director of the Global Varnasrama Educational Social Cultural Organization (GLOVESCO CAMBODIA)
Research Thesis: A Comparative Study of Traditional Educational Systems in India and Indonesia.

CONTENTS

ACKNOWLEDGMENT..3

APPRECIATIONS..4

CHAPTER ONE: ABRAHAMIC RELIGION

The Koran and Vedic literature are one in essence....................................12

The people of the book..14

Jacob's family resettled in Egypt..16

The Exodus from Egypt..17

The rise of Christianity..19

The rise of Islam..21

Paradise lost..24

CHAPTER TWO: THE MYSTERIES OF SCRIPTURES

An interfaith encounter 26

The holy Koran 29

The Vedic tradition 30

Evolution of consciousness 33

The Vedic Scriptures 38

CHAPTER THREE: A FAMILY CONFLICT

A battle between relatives 42

Declining to fight 44

Receiving supreme guidance 46

The concept of holy war 49

A gradual rise 52

For the sake of duty 55

CHAPTER FOUR: MOTIVATED RELIGION

Abraham was beyond religious affiliations 60

The collapse of past civilizations 62

Materially motivated religion 65

The lure of heavenly enjoyment 67

Concocted worship....................71

Beyond good work....................75

CHAPTER FIVE: THE ULTIMATE QUEST

A major test 77

Eternality in spirituality 78

Beyond the contaminated mind 80

CHAPTER SIX: WHEREVER YOU TURN IS HIS FACE

God directs everything....84

The all pervading Lord....86

I am indeed very near....88

Do not give likeness to Him....90

The parables of the slave and the dumb....92

CHAPTER SEVEN: THE SUPREME FRIEND

The allegory of the two companions....94

Individuality....100

A friend to all....107

The path of renunciation....110

CHAPTER EIGHT: THE KINGDOM OF GOD

The parables of the lantern and the fire 114

The abode of God contains many mansions 117

Devotional service 120

The Sincere 123

Spiritual Harmony 125

Bibliography 128

References 131

Chapter One
Abrahamic religion

The Koran and Vedic literature are one in essence

It may appear that the Koran and Vedic literature are conflicting in their precepts. Actually their essential principles are basically the same. God is one. Since God is one, His religion is also one.

Though the Koran and Vedic literature may seem different there are so many points of similarities that may not be easily detected. Differences arise not because of different scriptures; rather, they are caused by different levels of understanding. There is a need to realize that the goal is one; submission to the Supreme. The path is perfect, but we are not perfect. God is one, and when one is situated on that spiritual platform he can understand that there is no disagreement. The process of worship, though it may seem different, is also one. That process is to act for the pleasure of God and worship Him accordingly. The ultimate goal of different religious systems is to surrender to God. Since one may not be able to surrender to the will of God, different types of religious systems are needed. When one comes to the final state of obedience to God there is oneness in religion. Consequently, on the level of full surrender, there are no differences between the Koran and Vedic literature.

It is seen that differences exist even among the followers of a particular faith in the understanding of their own scriptures. Differences are not due to the content of the holy book itself. Differences exist because different kinds of thinkers have different spiritual conceptions. Differences of opinion arise due to the diversity in people's nature and experiences.

Different interpretations are manufactured according to one's level of perception, feelings, realizations and taste. People in general are motivated to gratify their personal longings. In this way different individual mentalities are displayed. One may be attached to a particular mistaken concept, and reject even a factual presentation that is contrary to his own understanding. The defect has not to be found in the Koran or in Vedic literature; rather, it is because people are attached to different aspects of the scriptures that suit their particular taste. One may even fervently believe that his version of understanding is the only real meaning of the scriptures. In this way differences are sometimes created.

It may seem that Vedic literatures contradict the teaching of Abraham, but it is not so. One will be astonished to learn that the original Vedic system scrupulously follows Abraham's principles as taught in the Koran. The reader may be surprised to learn that the final conclusion of both Vedic literature and Islam is to surrender to and worship the one Supreme Lord. Due to a lack of clarity in understanding the Koran and the Vedic texts may seem to have conflicting principles, but actually there is a great harmony between the Koran and Vedic teaching. They share a similar essence, which is the glorification, the worship and the acknowledgement of one Supreme God.

There is no doubt that both the Vedic system and the Koran are of divine origin. Their contents speak for themselves. The Vedas seem different, because its teachings give, as an option, a gradual process of how to reach pure monotheism. It may seem that Vedic knowledge does not stress monotheistic worship; however, the original Vedic system was highly monotheistic. True religion has to be purely monotheistic. The original Vedic tradition is monotheistic and it has very little to do with the modern conception known today as the Hindu religion. Hinduism is a foreign name. The words "Hindu" and "Hinduism" are not found in the Vedic literature, which favors the term sanātana-dharma meaning eternal occupation. This phrase elucidates that the natural occupation of the eternal soul is to serve God free from any artificial social or ethnic designations.

The true followers of the Vedic tradition are aware that both the Koran and the Vedic system share the same conception about God's absolute position. That was the conclusion of Shrī Chaitanya Mahāprabhu[1] who five hundred years ago showed that the Vedic conception is similar to that of the Koran. Genuine followers of the Vedic system, especially the Vaishnava school[2], have a strong conviction that the Vedic tradition and the Koran originate from the same Supreme Lord.

The truths of the Koran may appear to be easily comprehended, but they are actually very difficult to clearly understand. As stated in the Koran itself: *"None will grasp the message but men of understanding [Koran 2.269]"*. For instance, Muslim scholars are very much familiar with the concept of God as existing everywhere. However, the Koran mentions other aspects of God that are not very much known to a good number of scholars. This comparative study between the Vedic tradition and the Koran will be helpful for all seekers of truth to become more familiar with other concepts of God. It is meant to uphold harmonious understanding between the followers of the Vedic tradition and the Muslims about the Supreme Lord. It is a display of a unique exchange of thoughts between the Koran and Vedic literature.

The people of the book

Judaism, Christianity and Islam are known as Abrahamic religions. Islam accepts many aspects of Christianity and Judaism as part of its faith with some differences in interpretation and rejects other aspects. Muslims commonly refer to Jews and Christians as 'the People of the Book', people who were given similar teachings. The Hebrew scripture, the Torah, the Christian Bible and the Koran share a lot of histories, prophets, stories and teachings.

According to the Judeo, Christian and Muslim conception, around the 16th century BC, Judaism developed as the first major monotheistic religion. The history of Judaism begins with the covenant between God and Abraham. The nation of Israel descends from Abraham, through his son, Isaac. And the Arab nation descends from Abraham, through his son, Ishmael, whom Muslims believe to be a direct ancestor of Muhammad. Thus Ishmael is considered the father of the Arab nation and Isaac, the father of the Hebrews. Abraham married Sara, who gave birth to a son, named Isaac. Hagar, the second wife of Abraham, gave birth to a son named Ishmael. When Abraham prayed to God for a son, God gave him Ishmael. According to the Muslims, God tested Abraham's faith by asking him to sacrifice his only son, Ishmael. Just as Abraham was going to slaughter his only son, God praised him for his loyalty, and commanded him to sacrifice a ram instead. This led to the Muslim practice of slaughtering a ram once year in a festival known as *īd al adhā*.

Abraham had two sons, Ishmael, and Isaac. The son of Isaac, Jacob, moved from Canaan to Egypt with His twelve sons. After living many generations in Egypt the Hebrews became enslaved by the Pharaoh. Later Moses redeemed them from slavery and escaped the Pharaoh's hostilities. This was known as the Exodus journey out of Egypt. Once the Hebrews had settled in the Holy Land they established Saul as their first king. David was the second king. David's son, Solomon, became heir to the throne and built the First Hebrew Temple in Jerusalem. After Solomon's reign, the nation split into two kingdoms, the Kingdom of Israel in the north and the Kingdom of Judah in the south. The Kingdom of Israel was conquered by the Assyrian's in the late 8th century BCE. The Kingdom of Judah was conquered by the Babylonian army in the early 6th century BCE, destroying the First Temple that was built. A new Second Temple was later constructed. In 70 AD the Roman's destroyed this second Temple and Judaism fell apart. Following the destruction of Jerusalem Jewish worship went into exile, followed by the rise of Christianity.

Jacob's family resettled in Egypt

Jacob, the grandson of Abraham and Sara, and the son of Isaac, is the father of the twelve patriarchs or tribes of Israel. Jacob had twelve sons: Reuben, Simeon, Levi, Judah, Dan, Naphtali, Gad, Asher, Issachar, Zebulon, Joseph, and Benjamin. Later, Jacob is renamed 'Israel', the name after which the nation of Israel is named.

Due to a severe famine in Canaan, Jacob resettled his whole family in Egypt. Canaan was an ancient country in southwestern Asia on the east coast of the Mediterranean Sea; a place of pilgrimage for Christianity and Islam and Judaism. The history of how this happened is as follows: Jacob's son, Joseph, was sold as a slave to traders, who were heading to Egypt after his brothers, who were envious of him, threw him into a well. They were jealous of him because Jacob favored him and his brother, Benjamin, much more than them. He was rescued from the well by travelers in a caravan who were looking for water. When they reached Egypt, they sold Joseph as a slave to a rich merchant whose wife was very much attracted to Joseph. Joseph resisted the advances of his master's wife for a long time. Finally, she approached him with an offer of sexual favors, and then, accused him of trying to rape her. He was then thrown into prison.

After Joseph had spent a few years in prison, the Pharaoh of Egypt had two troubling dreams. His servant recalled having met Joseph, who successfully interpreted his dream when he was in Pharaoh's prison with Joseph. The Pharaoh called Joseph from prison and he fruitfully interpreted the Pharaoh's dreams: Joseph prophesized seven years each of abundance and famine. The Pharaoh was so impressed that he made Joseph his viceroy. Joseph became his second-in-command in Egypt and the manager of Egypt's grain stores. When the prophesied famine struck throughout the country, Joseph sold the stored grain to men of all nations.

Due to the severity of the famine, Jacob sent his ten sons, excluding Benjamin, to Egypt to procure grain for their starving families. Joseph recognized his brothers but did not reveal himself to them. Desiring them to bring his brother, Benjamin, to Egypt, Joseph accused them of being spies. He imprisoned Simeon, one of Joseph's ten brothers, as a hostage, and demanded them to bring Benjamin. When the famine worsened and food stores ran out, Jacob sent his sons again to Egypt, along with Benjamin. On meeting them, Joseph threatened to imprison Benjamin, but Judah offered himself in Benjamin's place. Overcome with emotion, Joseph revealed himself to his brothers and made arrangements for them to move Jacob's entire family to Egypt. In this way the whole family of Jacob settled very comfortably and happily in Egypt.

The Exodus from Egypt

After living many generations in Egypt the descendents of Jacob, the Jews, became enslaved by the Pharaoh. God later commanded Moses to redeem them from slavery, leading to the Exodus, a journey to escape the Pharaoh's hostilities.

Moses was born around 1228 B.C into a family of Hebrews living in Egypt. The Pharaoh soothsayers predicted the birth of a male child who would be the cause of the Pharaoh's downfall. The ruling Pharaoh thus ordered the killing of all new-born Hebrew males. To protect her son from the Pharaoh's wrath, Moses' mother put him in a basket and set him adrift on the Nile. He was discovered by the Pharaoh's wife, Asiya, who adopted him. He became a powerful statesman, second only to the Pharaoh. However, this changed when in rescuing a Hebrew, he accidentally killed an Egyptian. The Pharaoh then ordered the arrest of Moses, but he escaped into the desert. After travelling in the desert for a long time, he arrived at a place called Median. He then came into the company of Jethro, who recognized Moses as a saintly person. Jethro then arranged the marriage between Moses and his daughter, Zipporah, who then worked for his father-in-law for a few years. Moses then decided to return to Egypt. On his way back, he stopped at Mount Sinai and noticed a fire upon the mountain. When he came to the fire, he heard a voice calling him by name. *"O Moses, I am Your Lord [Koran 20:9]"*. The Lord ordered Moses to throw his walking stick onto the ground. As a sign to Moses from God the staff was transformed into a snake. Moses and his brother, Aaron, were ordered to embark for Egypt and face the Pharaoh. When Moses approached the Pharaoh, the Pharaoh replied, 'I am the living god'. He refused to submit to the instructions of God, as given by Moses. Severe plagues hit Egypt along with drought and famine. The people of Egypt become greatly distressed. Finally, the Pharaoh allowed Moses to take the Hebrews and go out from Egypt for good. However, news came to the Pharaoh that Moses and his people had lost their way in the Sinai desert. The Pharaoh changed his mind, thinking that God's favor had left Moses. He ordered the best of the Egyptian army to pursue the Hebrews to the shore of the sea to re-enslave them. The Lord split the sea providing a path for the Hebrews to cross over this overwhelming barrier. The Pharaoh used the miracle to deceive his soldiers into thinking that it was his god who had opened the sea for him so that he could follow the Hebrews and recapture them. As soon as the Jews safely reached the other side, the sea closed and the whole Egyptian army drowned. The Pharaoh's tyrannical strength was crushed.

Once the Hebrews had settled in the holy land, the place of worship for a Jewish congregation was planted. They established Saul as their king. "*The Lord has raised Saul as king over you [Koran 2:247]"*. He was the first king of the Jews who defended the Hebrews against many enemies, especially the Philistines. David was the second king of the Jews. It was David's son, Solomon, who became heir to the throne and built the First Hebrew Temple in Jerusalem. *"Solomon was David's heir [Koran 27:16]"*. After Solomon's reign, the nation split into two kingdoms: The Kingdom of Israel in the north and the Kingdom of Judah in the south. The Kingdom of Israel was conquered by the Assyrian ruler Sargon II in the late 8th century BCE. The Kingdom of Judah continued as an independent state until it was conquered by the Babylonian army in the early 6th century BCE. During this period, the First Temple which was the center of ancient Jewish worship was destroyed. The

Judean elite were exiled to Babylonia and this is regarded as the first dispersion of the Jews outside Israel. Later many of them returned to their homeland after the subsequent conquest of Babylonia by the Persians seventy years later. A new Second Temple was constructed, and old religious practices were resumed. The Jewish Second Temple was an important shrine which stood in Jerusalem between 516 BCE and 70 CE. It replaced the First Temple which was destroyed in 586 BCE, while the Jewish nation was exiled to Babylon. With their return to Jerusalem, construction started at the original site of Solomon's Temple, which had remained a devastated heap during approximately 70 years of captivity[3]. In 66 CE, because of Greek and Jewish religious tensions, the Jewish population rebelled against the Roman Empire. Later it grew with anti-taxation protests and attacks upon Roman citizens[4]. Four years later, in 70 CE, Roman legions retook and subsequently destroyed much of Jerusalem and the Second Temple. Although Jews continued to inhabit the destroyed city, Jerusalem was totally demolished in 135 CE.

The rise of Christianity

In its origin Christianity is most intimately connected with Judaism. The first disciples of Jesus were all Jews, either by birth or conversion. Jesus was Jewish, he preached to the Jewish people. Christianity started as a small Jewish sect[5]. It developed into a religion clearly distinct from Judaism several decades after Jesus' death. It took centuries for a complete break between Judaism and Christianity to manifest. Jewish Christians continued to worship in synagogues for centuries[6]. The split between Judaism and Christianity is usually attributed to a number of factors: The rejection of Jesus as a messiah in 30 AD, the destruction of the second temple in 70 AD, and the condemnation of Christians as heretic in the council of Jamnia in 90 AD[7]. By the end of the 1st century, Christianity began to be recognized as a separate religion from Judaism. When the Jews revolted against Rome, a number of Christians were still part of the Jewish community. However, they did not support or take part in the revolt against the Roman Empire. After the destruction of the Second Temple in 70 AD these

Christians left the Jewish community around this time. Breaking with Judaism, they became a separate religion. Moreover, the belief in a resurrected messiah is unacceptable to Jews who used this fact to explain the break between Judaism and Christianity.

Jesus and his apostles, disciples, and early followers traveled from Galilee to the Jewish Temple in Jerusalem in 33 AD. At that time the second temple was not yet destroyed. Jerusalem was under the Roman occupation. After an incident in the Temple, Jesus was crucified. According to Christian belief, he rose again and then ascended to heaven with a prophecy to return. Jerusalem was the first center of the church[8]. The apostles lived and taught there for some time. Jesus' brother James and other family members held leadership positions in the surrounding area after the destruction of Jerusalem when all Jews were banished from the city[9]. After the death of Jesus, Jerusalem became the head-quarters of the apostles, the original twelve disciples chosen by Christ to preach his gospel. They became the leaders of the newly formed religious movement with about a hundred followers, followed by the early bishops, whom Christians considered the successors of the apostles.

At the time of Jesus Christ the world was largely under the dominion of the Roman Empire. Despite the rule of the Roman Empire, Christianity began to spread quite rapidly around 30 AD. From the beginning, Christians were subject to persecution at the hands of the authorities of the Roman Empire. State persecution ceased in the 4th century. In 380 AD Emperor Theodosius I enacted a law establishing Christianity as the official religion of the Roman Empire. By the end of the 1st century, Christianity became the favored religion of the Roman Empire, as well as a significant religion outside the empire[10]. The Christian Church prevailed over Paganism[11]. The Roman Empire controlled approximately 6.5 million km^2 of land surface. The Empire's vast extent included large territorial holdings in Europe and around the Mediterranean[12]. With the rise of Christianity countries known today as Portugal, Spain, France, Monaco, Montenegro, Belgium, Netherlands, Luxembourg, Germany, Switzerland, Italy, Vatican City, San Marino, Austria , Liechtenstein, United Kingdom, Hungary , Bulgaria,

Romania , Slovenia , Slovakia , Greece, Cyprus , Albania, Andorra, Armenia, Azerbaijan, Bosnia, Herzegovina, Croatia , Georgia, Kosovo, Macedonia Moldova, Serbia, Ukraine, Morocco , Algeria, Tunisia, Libya, Egypt, Turkey, Iran, Iraq, Kuwait, Syria, Saudi Arabia, Israel, Palestine, Lebanon, and Jordan all became Christians.

The rise of Islam

Islam originated in Arabia in the early 7th century. From the 7th century onwards, the followers of Islam conquered many Christian lands that were under the domination of the Roman Empire. It is a monotheistic Abrahamic religion based on the teachings of the Koran and the prophet Muhammad (570–632). Muslims believe that God revealed his final message to humanity through Muhammad via the archangel Gabriel. Muhammad was a religious, political, and military leader who was the founder of Islam. The term 'Islam' is translated as peace, submission, a total surrender of oneself to God and submission to His will. The Koran states that the name Muslim was given by Abraham. *"It is the cult of your father Abraham. It is he who named you Muslims [22:78]"*. Muslims regard Islam as a monotheistic faith meant for all men, revealed to Adam, Abraham, Moses, Jesus, and other prophets. For them, Muhammad was God's final prophet and the Koran is the holy book of revelations he received.

The Koran states that all Muslims must believe in God, his revelations, his angels, his messengers, and in the "Day of Judgment"[13]. The Koran states that resurrection will be followed by the gathering of mankind, culminating in their judgment by God[14]. Muslims view heaven as a paradise of uninterrupted enjoyment, with Koranic references describing its features and the sensual pleasures to come. There are also references to an everlasting abode where the believer will remain forever. This is described as the supreme achievement beyond the joy of paradise. "*Allah has promised to men and women who believe; gardens with stream of running water where they will abide forever and beautiful mansions in gardens of everlasting bliss. But the greatest bliss is the good pleasure of Allah: that is the supreme felicity [Koran 9:72]".*

The pillars of Islam are five essential practices:

1. Islam's fundamental theological concept is *tawhīd*, the belief that there is only one God. *Tawhīd* is expressed in the *shahāda*, testification, which declares that there is only one Supreme God, and that Muhammad is God's messenger. The *shahāda*, which is the basic tenet of Islam: "*ashhadu anna-lā ilāha ilā llāhu wa ashadu anna muhammadan rasūlu-llāh*", "I testify that there is none worthy of worship except Allah and I testify that Muhammad is the Messenger of God." This testament is a foundation for all other beliefs and practices in Islam. Muslims must repeat the *shahāda* in prayer, and non-Muslims wishing to convert to Islam are required to recite this statement at the time of their conversion[15].

2. Salāt, or ritual prayer, which must be performed five times a day. Each *salāt*, prayer, is done facing towards the Kāba, the Holy Mosque, in Mecca. *Salāt* is intended to focus the mind on God, and is seen as a personal communication with Him that expresses gratitude and worship. The prayers are recited in the Arabic language, and consist of verses from the Koran[16].

3. Zakāt or alms-giving: This is the practice of giving based on one's accumulated wealth, and is obligatory for all Muslims who can afford it. A fixed portion is given to help the poor or needy, and to distribute the teachings of Islam[17].

4. *Sawm* or fasting: Muslims must not eat, drink even water or have sexual intercourses from dawn to dusk during the month of *Ramadān*. The fast is to encourage a feeling of nearness to God. For fasting, flexibility is allowed depending on the circumstances[18].

5. The *Hajj*[19] is the pilgrimage to the city of Mecca. Every Muslim who can afford it must make the pilgrimage to Mecca at least once in his or her life time. When the pilgrim is about ten kilometers from Mecca, he must dress in *Ihrām*, clothing, which consists of two white seamless sheets. Rituals of the *Hajj* include walking seven times around the Holy Mosque, touching the Black Stone, running seven times between Mount *Safa* and Mount *Marwah*, and symbolically stoning the Devil in Mina. The pilgrim is honored in his or her community, although Islamic teachers say that the pilgrimage should be an expression of devotion to God instead of a means to gain social standing. Many practices fall into the category of Islamic etiquette. This includes greeting others with "*as-salāmu alaykum*", "peace be unto you", saying "*bismillah*", "in the name of God," before meals, and using only the right hand for eating and drinking. Islamic hygienic practices mainly fall into the category of personal cleanliness and health, such as the circumcision of male offspring. Islamic burial rituals include saying the "*salāt aljanāzah*", "funeral prayer" over the bathed and enshrouded dead body, and burying it in a grave. Muslims are restricted in their diet. Prohibited foods include pork products, blood, the dead and rotting body of an animal, and alcohol. All meat must come from an animal slaughtered in the name of God by a Muslim. Food permissible for Muslims is known as *halāl* or lawful food.

Paradise lost

In Islam, Adam is considered the first Prophet of God, who according to the Koran was the first man and the progenitor of the human race. Muslims claim that Islam is the original religion of the world, because Adam was the first living being who took birth on earth.

The account in the Koran records that God first fashioned Adam out of "the dust of the ground" and then "breathed into him His Spirit". *"I have fashioned him and breathed into him of My spirit [Koran 38:71]".* God then placed Adam and Eve in a heavenly garden, giving him the commandment to not approach the tree. On the day that he should approach that tree he shall run into harm and transgression. "*We said to Adam both you and your spouse live in the Garden, eat freely to your fill whatever you like, but approach not this tree or you will become transgressor [Koran 2: 35]".* When they disobeyed the Lord's commandment, Adam and Eve were subsequently expelled from the heavenly garden. They lost their immortality after they broke God's law. This occurred after Satan tempted them. "*Satan suggested, 'Your Lord has forbidden you to go near this tree that you may not become angels or immortal.' [Koran 7:20]".* Satan had lured Adam and Eve into disobeying God. This was the first act of revenge from Satan against Adam. He took revenge because when God created Adam, He asked the angels and Satan to bow down to Adam. Satan refused. He was then banished from heaven. As a result of their disobedience to God, Adam and Eve became aware of the fact that they were naked. Shame became manifest to them. "*Their Lord called unto them: 'Did I not forbid you that tree, and tell you that Satan was an avowed enemy unto you?' [Koran 7:22]".* As a result of their breaking God's law, the couple was expelled from the garden and both received a curse. *"Allah said, 'get down with enmity to each other. On earth will be your dwelling place and your means of livelihood for a while [Koran7:24]".* The Koran mentions that Adam was misled by deception and was in fact pardoned by God after much repentance *"Then Adam received (some) words from his Lord, so He turned to him mercifully [Koran 2:37]."*

There is no mention in the Koran about the location of the Paradise where Adam and Eve were dwelling. Some think that they were in heaven. Others reject this theory because if it was heaven Satan would have been forbidden to enter. They either think that it is another paradise that was created by God for Adam and Eve or they think that it is a paradise on the earth.

Chapter Two
The mysteries of scriptures

An interfaith encounter

To grow in understanding, respectful communication between opposing parties is needed. Willingness to exchange different ideas is also helpful in one's own personal spiritual journey. For this it is necessary to put aside any preconceived ideas and first hear with an open mind. Hostility, prejudice, hate, anger and a defensive attitude should be avoided, for they cause withdrawal, alienation, unfriendliness and division. Humility, gratitude, honesty, sincerity and a sense of compassion are indispensable for a constructive exchange of views.

Five hundred years ago a great interesting interreligious dialogue took place between Śrī Chaitanya Mahāprabhu and a great saintly Muslim. Śrī Chaitanya Mahāprabhu was known at that time as a great saint who spread the congregational recitation of the holy names of the Lord as the primary means to realize pure love of God. He was also recognized as one of the greatest Vedic scholarrs of his time. He was very fond of reading the Koran in its original and purest form in the Arabic language. Śrī Chaitanya Mahāprabhu could fluently speak and read Arabic and Persian. Krishna dāsa Kavirāja Goswami, a great saintly contemporary of Śrī Chaitanya Mahāprabhu, compiled the great scripture Shri Chaitanya Charitamrita[20], which is regarded as the most authoritative text on Śrī Chaitanya Mahāprabhu's life and teachings. The following statements are recorded there.

One day a great Muslim scholar met Shrī Chaitanya Mahāprabhu in the western part of India, on the way to Prayāga, on the path along the banks of the Ganges[21]. Upon seeing Shrī Chaitanya Mahāprabhu, the heart of that great saintly Muslim was attracted. That Muslim saint wanted to talk to Shrī Chaitanya Mahāprabhu and establish on the basis of the Koran that God is impersonal [CC Madhya 18.186]. Being very much conversant with the divine message of the holy Koran Shrī Chaitanya Mahāprabhu was very much surprised to hear that the final conclusion of the saintly person is the impersonal conception of God. When that saintly person tried to establish, on the authority of the Koran, that God was formless, Shrī Chaitanya Mahāprabhu challenged his argument [CC Madhya 18.187]. Whatever arguments he put forward, Shrī Chaitanya Mahāprabhu disproved them all. Finally the saintly person became stunned and could not speak [CC Madhya 18.188][22].

Shrī Chaitanya Mahāprabhu said to the saintly Muslim: The Koran certainly establishes that God is formless, but at the end it refutes the conception that God is formless and establishes that God is a person [CC Madhya 18.189]. The Koran accepts the fact that ultimately there is only one God. He is full of opulence [CC Madhya 18.190]. According to the Koran, the Lord has a supreme, blissful, transcendental body. He is the Absolute Truth, the all-pervading, omniscient and eternal being. He is the origin of everything [CC Madhya 18.191]. Creation, maintenance and dissolution come from Him. He is the original shelter of all gross and subtle cosmic manifestations [CC Madhya 18.192]. The Lord is the Supreme Truth, worshipable by everyone. He is the cause of all causes. By engaging in His devotional service, the living entity is relieved from material existence [CC Madhya 18.193][23].

He is the Absolute Truth, the all-pervading, omniscient and eternal being. He is the origin of everything. Creation, maintenance and dissolution come from Him. He is the original shelter of all gross and subtle cosmic manifestations. The Lord is the Supreme Truth, worshipable by everyone. He is the cause of all causes. By engaging in His devotional service, the living entity is relieved from material existence. No conditioned soul can get out of material bondage without serving the Supreme Lord. Love for Him is the ultimate goal of life. In the Koran there are descriptions of fruitive activities, speculative knowledge, mystic power and union with the Supreme, but ultimately all these are refuted and the Lord's personal feature is established, along with His devotional service [CC Madhya 18.196]. Most scholars of the Koran are not very advanced in knowledge. Although there are many methods prescribed, they do not know that the ultimate conclusion should be considered the most powerful [CC Madhya 18.197]. Seeing your own Koran and deliberating over what is written there, what is your conclusion [CC Madhya 18.198]?"

The saintly Muslim replied, "All that you have said is true. This has certainly been written in the Koran, but most of our scholars can neither understand nor accept it [CC Madhya 18.199]. Usually they describe the Lord's impersonal aspect, but they hardly know that the Lord's personal feature is worshipable. They are undoubtedly lacking this knowledge [CC Madhya 18.200]. I have studied the Koran very extensively, but from it I cannot conclusively decide what the ultimate goal of life is or how I can approach it [CC Madhya 18.202]. Saying this, the saintly Muslim requested Śrī Caitanya Mahāprabhu to speak of life's ultimate goal and the process by which it could be obtained.

Many questions can be raised. Does the Koran contain fruitive activities, speculative knowledge, mystic power and devotional service? This book will gradually answer all these questions by giving Koranic references. First of all we will explain the history of the Koran and Vedic knowledge. Later, we will show that the Koran does contain different paths of religion such as fruitive activities, speculative knowledge, mystic power and ultimately devotional service to the Supreme Lord just as Vedic literatures do.

The holy Koran

The Koran literally means recitation. The language of the Koran is Arabic. To Muslims, the Koran is perfect only as revealed in the original Arabic. Translations are not regarded as the Koran itself because of the fallibility of translators and the impossibility of preserving the original inspired style. Muslims and even non-Muslim scholars of Islam universally acclaim the Koran as representative of the purest and most elegant forms of the Arabic language. The unexcelled literary style of Koranic Arabic is one of the proofs of its divine origin[24].

The Koran is venerated by all Muslims. There are no weaknesses and contradictions in it. It contains one hundred and fourteen chapters, which contain 6,236 *āyāt*, or verses. The Koran was revealed to Muhammad through the angel Gabriel on many occasions during a period of 23 years from 609 to 632, the year of his death[25]. The divine revelations were manifested through divine inspiration, which Muhammad sometimes uttered in the presence of his companions[26]. Muhammad's words were preserved and passed on through oral tradition of the Arabic culture[27]. The followers of Muhammad memorized and documented the divine messages delivered to him on makeshift material, such as palm leaves, fragments of pottery and on the shoulder blades of camels[28]. Some forty years after the passing away of Muhammad, they were transcribed in the written form that has been preserved to date without change[29]. Muhammad's life and death marked the end of prophecy since his prophetic mission satisfied for all time any need or demand for another prophet[30].

The Koran, for Muslims, is the final word of God. It contains His divine message to mankind as revealed to Muhammad. This divine communication is seen as the final stage in a long series of divine messages conducted through specific messengers or prophets chosen by God, starting with Adam and ending with Muhammad. For Muslims, Islam begins with Adam and Abraham. Along with his son, Ishmael, Abraham rebuilt what is now Mecca, the first temple in the world for the worship of God. For Muslims, Islam is the original religion that is going all the way back to Adam, who was the first prophet sent by God. Muhammad is the last of a long line of prophets, including Noah, Abraham, Moses, David, and Jesus. Muslims believe that Moses, David, Jesus, and others were prophets sent from God. They also believe that God delivered the Torah to Moses, and later, the Gospel to Jesus, but that they were later corrupted by their followers. Muslims accept the Torah, Psalms, and Gospels as revelations from God, but that some of these books and revelations had been lost or corrupted before the revelation of the Koran. According to Muslim conviction, the only authentic and complete book of God in existence today is the Koran. It has been preserved as it was revealed to Muhammad through the archangel, Gabriel, in its immaculate, pure form.

Muslims accept all Messengers of God, without any discrimination among them, as every known nation has a messenger from God. They were chosen by God to teach humanity and deliver His Divine message. The Koran mentions the name of some of them such as Adam, Noah, Abraham, Ishmael, Isaac, Jacob, Joseph, Job, Moses, Aaron, David, Solomon, Elias, Jonah, John the Baptist, and Jesus.

In Islam, prophets are men selected by God to be his messengers. Muslims believe that prophets are human and not divine. Although Islam teaches that Jesus was a prophet, Muslims do not believe that he was the Son of God, that he was divine. According to Muslims, Jesus was a human prophet who brought to the world a deeper understanding of the relationship between man, God and all living beings. Although Muslims believe that Jesus was a prophet, they reject the Christian doctrine of the Trinity, comparing it to polytheism. God is described in the Koran as *"He beget not, nor is He begotten; And there is none like unto Him [Koran 112:3-4]."*

The Vedic tradition

The word 'Vedas' mean knowledge. The Vedic scriptures are vast in scope[31]. The Ṛg Veda alone contains 1,017 hymns, the Mahābhārata consists of 110,000 couplets, and the eighteen chief Purāṇas contain hundreds of thousands of verses. The main purpose of the

Vedic literature is to impart the knowledge of how to become free from suffering through spiritual enlightenment. Its goal is to attain full realization of God, to realize the ultimate truth which leads to the ultimate freedom in the Kingdom of God.

The Vedic system strives not for academic knowledge for its own sake, but for the transformation of one's consciousness from material to spiritual. Despite its apparent joys, material life means suffering. The purpose of Vedic knowledge is to free the sincere inquirer from the suffering of birth, death, old age, and disease. Apart from these miseries, the Vedic writings describe another threefold set of miseries: miseries arising from the body and the mind, miseries inflicted by other beings such as humans, mosquitoes and beasts, and miseries arising from natural disturbances such as severe cold, heat, flood, earthquake, or drought.

The Vedic literature teaches that no one can find happiness in the material world. The forces of time and death force everyone to leave whatever is acquired through a lifetime's undertaking. Indeed, the earth is described as a place of death, a temporary place full of miseries [Bg. 8:15]. Yet, the Vedic philosophy does not put forth a pessimistic and fatalistic rejection of the world, but, rather; a positive God centered existence. A spiritual life based on one's eternal spiritual identity is presented to realize eternal spiritual happiness in relation to God, even while still living in this temporary, miserable world. The Vedic system offers an opportunity to inquire about oneself and the Supreme Lord and revive one's eternal loving relationship with God.

According to the Vedic tradition, the Vedic literatures are absolute and self-authoritative. *"Devotional service of the Lord that ignores the authorized Vedic literatures like the Upanișhads, Purāṇas and Nārada-pañcarātra is simply an unnecessary disturbance in society (Bhakti-rasāmṛta-sindhu 1.2.101)."* Vedic literatures depend on nothing but themselves for explanation because they are directly revealed by the Lord. *"The Vedas are directly manifested from the infallible Supreme Lord [Bg. 3:15]"*. Since human beings are limited and imperfect, their perception, theories, and speculations cannot be perfect. The Vedic process of learning is to receive knowledge by hearing from the highest authority, which is coming directly from God and handed down without change through the chain of disciplic succession of spiritual teachers.

To cite a traditional example, if a child wants to know who his father is, he should ask his mother, who is considered the only authority who can say who the father is. To find his father, he may make a survey of the entire male population, but he cannot reach everyone. To actually know who his father is, he must ask his mother, the final authority on the matter. As the mother is the only authority to identify the father of a child, so the Mother Vedas, which are delivered directly from the Lord, are the genuine spiritual authority.

The Vedic conception of authority refers to a person who receives perfect knowledge from the perfect Supreme Lord. One who receives perfect knowledge from the Supreme Lord and transmits that knowledge to others without any change and misinterpretation attains the highest perfectional stage of salvation. For instance, Vedic knowledge was imparted to Brahmā through oral reception. Indeed, Brahmā received the knowledge directly from the Supreme Lord, who then instructed it to his son Nārada, whose realizations appear throughout Vedic literature. And Nārada instructed it to His disciple, the sage Vyāsadeva. Thus, the message of Vedic literature descends through a chain of disciplic succession that is still present today. Formerly Vedic scripture came down by word of mouth from teachers to their disciples, but thousands of years ago, the sage Vyāsadeva compiled all the Vedic scriptures in written form.

Hearing God's message is imperative when one inquires about subject matter beyond the purview of one's limited senses and power of reason. One cannot get perfect knowledge by direct perception, pratyakṣa, or by the inductive method, anumāna. The process of direct perception, pratyakṣa, is imperfect. For example, to our eyes the sun may seem no larger than a coin, but we learn that our senses mislead us, for the sun is actually many times larger than the earth. The inductive method, anumāna means I cannot see directly, but by the symptoms I can imagine. Just like there is some sound on the roof. And someone who is not on the roof will conjecture about that sound thinking that it may be a cat or some burglar. That is anumāna. But a person who is on the roof can explain the exact nature of that sound, and that is perfect knowledge. Since human beings are limited and imperfect the best process for coming to a decisive conclusion for any subject matter is to receive that knowledge by hearing from the highest authority. The Vedic system coming directly from God, through a chain of disciplic succession is considered this highest authority.

Evolution of consciousness

The aim of the Vedic system is to elevate one from a state of ignorance to a state of pure goodness. Ignorance is opposed to goodness. In ignorance, affected by lust, hate and greed, one becomes illusioned. An illusioned man cannot understand what is what. Instead of advancing in spiritual revelation, one becomes more and more degraded. In ignorance, one does not possess perfect wisdom nor does he know what real enjoyment is. Bewildered by his passions, one strives for pleasure that results in suffering. Only in goodness one is able to see things as they are for one's true benefit.

There are five distinct levels of awareness: namely veiled, shrunken, budding, blooming, and fully bloomed consciousness. On the true spiritual path, these different five grades of covering that act like veils are progressively dissolved, ultimately revealing one's true consciousness. For instance, in the early morning, sometimes due to the fog, the sky is not seen. But as soon as the sun rises on the horizon, the fog, which has no permanent existence, disappears. It comes into being for some time, and then vanishes. But the sky and the sun always exist. Similarly, the consciousness of the soul is sometimes obscured by different coverings but cannot be destroyed. "*As fire is covered by smoke, as a mirror is covered by dust, or as the embryo is covered by the womb, the living entity is similarly covered by different degrees of material desires [Bg.3.38]*".

Consciousness pervades the entire body. As the sun, although situated in one place, fills the universe with light, similarly the soul fills the body with consciousness. As the fragrance of flowers travel to a place far from its source, similarly the consciousness that emanates from the soul spreads throughout the body, and is never separated from its source, the soul. *"That which pervades the entire body you should know to be indestructible. No one is able to destroy that imperishable soul [Bg.2.17]".* Everyone is conscious of the pains and pleasures of his body. This is due to the presence of the soul. The pains and pleasures of one body are unknown to another. Therefore, within each and every body is an individual separate soul.

Consciousness may be reflected by the covering of material conditions. As white light reflected through colored glasses may appear to be red, blue or yellow. Once these colored glasses are taken away the white light is no longer distorted. Similarly, material activities cover one's original consciousness and spiritual activities revive one's original consciousness. *"Whose eyes had been under a cover from remembrance of Me and they could not even hear [Koran 18:101]".* As by digging a well, water is brought forth but not created, so by spiritual activities the true nature of the soul is reawakened. The dirt that veils a jewel prevents it from being appreciated in its full glory. Washing the dirt that covers a jewel uncovers its true splendor. So, by removing the dirt of materialistic consciousness, the soul's pure qualities manifest. The soul's splendor is not created, but it is merely revived.

The following Koranic verse speaks about the evolution of consciousness. *"God has sealed their hearts and ears and veiled their eyes [Koran 2:7]".* This sealing of the heart and ear and veiling of the eyes describes this covering of consciousness. The goal of the Koran is to clear up one's consciousness from these different degrees of covering. Water is clear, but if toxic chemicals are added its pure quality becomes spoiled. No benefit is derived from drinking such water. Likewise, when a person's consciousness is covered, one can neither derive true satisfaction in his activities nor peace of mind. For true satisfaction, the Koran recommends the process for the true evolution of consciousness. Full enlightenment of the soul is possible once God removes this sealing of the heart and ear and veiling of the eyes. Evolution towards perfection begins when there is a transition from identification with matter to spirit. A veiled consciousness is considered material where one sees oneself separate from God. In developed consciousness one's spiritual relationship with God is experienced.

According to Vedic literature, if one follows its precepts, one evolves through five distinct levels of awareness: namely veiled, shrunken, budding, blooming, and fully bloomed consciousness. This is called the evolution of consciousness. In the first level called veiled consciousness one is food conscious. A child or an animal is satisfied only by getting nice food. One's only concern is simply eating and sleeping. The Vedic teaching and the Koran's goal are to elevate one from food consciousness level to enlightened consciousness. The following Koranic verse explains this veiled consciousness. *"Eat and enjoy for a little while [Koran 77:46]"*. According to the Vedic system, persons who are only engaged in planning a higher standard of materialistic life consisting of eating and mating are no better than animals. *"Both animals and men share the activities of eating, sleeping, mating and defending. But the special property of the human is that they are able to engage in spiritual life. Therefore without spiritual life, humans are on the level of animals [Hitopadesh]."*

In the second level, which is shrunken consciousness, one is aware that he exists. In the first level one is only food conscious. Here one's consciousness is higher. One is aware of his body and he wants to protect it from any possible danger. If one can continue his life without being destroyed one thinks himself happy. In the bodily concept of life, one understands life to be meant for sense enjoyment. Identification with the body and acting on the bodily platform is the cause of troublesome life. One simply wants to enjoy his senses and all his activities are centered on this purpose. On this level of consciousness, one cannot tolerate any bodily inconveniences. To gratify his senses and attain material comforts a person will work like a beast of burden. Such people won't lift a finger for the service of God.

In the Koran there is a detailed description of some believers who did not want to do their duty for the Lord's service. There was too much heat in the desert. They were unwilling to leave their home and use their wealth for God. *"Not a penny did they spend, nor did they traverse a land [Koran 9:121]". "The hypocrites did not experience any hardship, thirst, fatigue and hunger in the service of God. No harm did they receive from the enemy [Koran 9:120]"*. In shrunken consciousness one is unwilling to engage his earnings and energies for God. One simply wants to enjoy the fruits of his work for his own sensual gratification. Such a person is called a fruitive worker. In the Vedas, Arjuna, at first, refused to do his duty. *"O maintainer of all living entities, I am not prepared to fight with them even in exchange for the three worlds, let alone this earth [Bg. 1.35]".*

In the third level, budding consciousness, one realizes that large amounts of material possessions cannot give real happiness. From excessive engagement in sensual enjoyment, frustration arises. At this time, one is no longer eager to work like a beast to acquire material possessions. He becomes inquisitive to understand the cause of his suffering. When one progresses from the bodily platform, one reaches the mental platform. One has a philosophical approach for the values of life. At that time the mind becomes the center of sensual activities. One identifies the mind with the self.

Budding consciousness is shown in the following Koranic verse. *"When will you realize that, 'Of no profit to me has been my wealth' [Koran 69:28]"?* This Koranic verse stresses the fact that wealth alone does not give one full satisfaction. From this point one reaches a higher platform of spiritual inquiry. Such process is known as the philosophical search for truth. *"All occupational engagements are certainly meant for ultimate salvation. They should never be performed for material gain. Furthermore, according to sages, one who is engaged in the ultimate occupational service should never use material gain to cultivate sense gratification. Life's desires should never be directed toward sense gratification. One should desire only a healthy life, or self-preservation, since a human being is meant for inquiry about the Absolute Truth. Nothing else should be the goal of one's works [SB 1.2.9-10]".*

Every human has the potential to inquire as to the nature of life: "Why am I here? Who am I? Where did I come from? Where am I going?" That becomes the most important thing in his life. Everything else becomes secondary. Those who begin to question why they are suffering, where they came from and where they shall go after death are beyond the platform of the beast. This is the beginning of human life[32]. At that time one progresses from the bodily platform to the mental platform which is characterized by a philosophical search for the understanding of the true nature of one's existence. Instead of being a fruitive worker, who wants just to enjoy the fruit of his work, one comes to the platform of speculative knowledge[33]. On the platform of speculative knowledge, one is considered thousands times better than the fruitive worker whose main goal is only bodily enjoyment.

In the fourth level, one rises above the mental platform to an intellectual understanding that he is not this body but pure spirit soul. By the evolutionary process of philosophical life, he is situated in the fourth stage of blooming consciousness. This understanding that one is spirit soul is all important. By such realization one becomes free from suffering. As the Vedas confirm, he who knows the soul surpasses grief[34]. On the intellectual platform one is called a mystic[35]. A mystic is one who is initiated into the mysteries of higher knowledge.

Mysticism is a process that is performed through contemplation on the Supreme. By the realization that God is very near, the mystic surpasses grief, and attains the stage of blooming consciousness. The chief cause of suffering is negligence of our connection with God. Feeling the nearness of God, the mystic establishes union with Him. Blooming consciousness is described in the following Koranic verse. *"I am indeed very near and listen to the prayer of every suppliant when he calls [Koran 2:186]".* A close communion is established when the mystic practically feels that the Lord listens to his prayers. *"For one who has conquered the mind, the Supreme Spirit is already reached, for he has attained tranquility [Bg.6.7]".*

One, who controls his mind by fixing it on the Supreme, subdues his material desires and understands one's spiritual nature feels that the Lord is always near.

The ultimate perfection comes with the fifth level which is the fully bloomed consciousness. When a person loses interest in the paths of fruitive activities, speculative knowledge and mysticism, one comes to the path of devotional service. This is the highest development of human consciousness. In the fully bloomed consciousness there is no scope for fruitive activities, which are meant for sense enjoyment. Even speculative knowledge, which is meant for detachment from worldly activities, and mysticism, where one has realized that God is near are not the final goal. In devotional service one develops his relationship with God and constantly remembers and serves Him with full devotion. Fully bloomed consciousness is put forward in the following Koranic and Vedic verses. *"Who remembers Allah while standing, sitting and lying on their sides, and who reflects on the creation of the heavens and the earth: "Our Lord! You have not created this in vain! Glory unto You! [Koran 3:191]". "Always chanting My glories, endeavoring with great determination, bowing down before Me, these great souls perpetually worship Me with devotion [Bg.9.14]".*

As it is said in Vedic literature, the Supreme Lord and the living entities are both joyful by nature[36]. However, in the lower four stages of life, namely veiled, shrunken, budding, and even in blooming consciousness, one's consciousness is still affected by many material anxieties. This stage of fully bloomed consciousness is explained in the Vedic system as the stage of life where there is no anxiety and no hankering. This stage begins when one becomes equally disposed toward all living entities, and when one always hankers to render service unto the Supreme Lord[37].

The Vedic Scriptures

The Vedic scriptures are compiled with full explanation of these five levels of consciousness. Different sections of the Vedic literatures are given to each one according to the level of one's consciousness. The Vedic system seems to be very puzzling. How one can appreciate the final level, if one's consciousness is situated in a lower one? Different parts of the Vedic teaching focuses on different processes for different categories of people. In the first level of veiled consciousness, books about spirits, black arts, and black magic are given. In the second level of shrunken consciousness, the four Vedic literatures, namely the *Ṛg Veda*, *Yajur Veda*, *Sāma Veda*, and *Atharva Veda* are recommended. In this platform one is situated on the path of fruitive activities. In third level of budding consciousness, the *Upaniṣhads* are advocated. In this platform one is situated on the path of speculative knowledge. In fourth level of blooming consciousness the *Vedānta-sūtra* is recommended. In this platform one is situated on the path of mysticism. And in the fifth level of fully bloomed consciousness, *Śrīmad-Bhāgavatam*, which directly reveals the glories of the Supreme Lord and His devotional service, is given. In this platform one is situated on the path of devotional service to the Supreme Lord.

There are particular recommendations recommended in the scriptures for fruitive activities, speculative knowledge, mysticism and devotional service. For fruitive activities the four Vedic literatures, namely the *Ṛg Veda*, *Yajur Veda*, *Sāma Veda*, and *Atharva Veda* encourage satisfaction of material desires through worship of the gods. This path of fruitive activities is inferior, for real life begins when one pursues one's true spiritual existence. One who is not firmly fixed in true knowledge is diverted by various types of fruitive acts. When there is no longer attraction to heavenly sensual enjoyment manifested in fruitive activities, one is gradually elevated from the field of sense gratification to a spiritual position.

The *Upaniṣhads* transcend the sections for fruitive activities described in the four Vedic literatures. The *Upaniṣhads* teach that the true aim of life is the release from material suffering through the development of spiritual knowledge. The religious aim is no longer the obtaining of earthly and heavenly happiness by sacrificing correctly to the gods. "Why am I here? Who am I? Where did I come from? Where am I going?" That becomes the most important thing in life.

The *Upanishads* are a collection of 108 philosophical dissertations. The essence of all the *Upanishads* is the *Vedānta-sūtra* which consists of codes revealing the method of understanding Vedic knowledge. A sutra is a code that expresses the essence of all knowledge in a minimum of words. It must be universally applicable and faultless in its linguistic presentation. *Vedānta* comprises the purport of the *Upanishads*, which are part of Vedic knowledge. Veda means "knowledge" and anta means "the end," therefore it can be understood that *Vedānta* provides the correct understanding of the ultimate purpose of the Vedic literatures.

The *Ṛg Veda, Yajur Veda, Sāma Veda,* and *Atharva Veda* are very difficult to understand. To make them easily understandable, these four Vedic literatures are again explained in the *Mahābhārata*, the *Rāmāyaṇa* and the eighteen *Purāṇas*. In this format the teachings are presented in the form of stories and historical incidents so that the common men can grasp them without difficulty. *"There are eighteen major Purāṇas: Brahma, Padma, Viṣṇu, Śiva, Linga, Garuḍa, Nāradīya, Bhāgavata, Agni, Bhaviṣya, Skandha, Brahma-Vaivarta, Markaṇḍeya, Vāmana, Varāha, Matsya, Kūrma, and Brahmāṇḍa (SB 12.7.23-24)". The Purāṇas in the mode of goodness glorify the Supreme Lord, Śrī Kṛṣṇa; those in the mode of passion promote the glories of the god Brahmā; and those in the mode of ignorance celebrate the greatness of the gods Agni, Śiva, and Dūrga. In addition many other scriptures have different mixtures of goodness, passion, and ignorance, and promote the worship of gods like Sarasvatī and Lakṣmī along with worship of ancestors, and many other lower religious processes[38]".*

As the Vedic rituals are hard to understand and the *Vedānta-sūtra* is condensed and highly philosophical, the *Śrīmad-Bhāgavatam* is given because it directly reveals the glories of the Supreme Lord and His devotional service. *Śrīmad-Bhāgavatam* is beyond ignorance and even mundane goodness. It is meant for those who are situated in devotional service to the Supreme Lord and to bring others to that platform. *Śrīmad—Bhāgavatam* is considered the direct commentary on the *Vedānta-sūtra*. Of all the *Purāṇas*, the *Bhāgavata Purāṇa* or *Śrīmad-Bhāgavatam* is the foremost. "*Vyāsadeva* collected the essence of the four *Vedas* and *Upaniṣads*, and composed them in the form of codes called the *Vedāntasūtras*. In *Vedānta-sūtra* the purpose of all Vedic knowledge is explained, and in *Śrīmad-Bhāgavatam*, it is elaborated upon in 18,000 verses. What is explained in *Śrīmad-Bhāgavatam* and in the *Upaniṣads* serves the same purpose (*Cc. Madhya* 25.98-100)." "The essence of all Vedic literature, the *Vedas, Purāṇas, and Itihasas,* has been collected in the *Śrīmad-Bhāgavatam*[39]".

Chapter Three
A family conflict

A battle between relatives

In the Koran as well as in the Bhagavad-gītā, a battle among relatives took place. When Muhammad received the revelation in Mecca, his family was antagonist to his message. At first Muhammad was protected by his uncle. But when his uncle died, some members of his family persecuted him. In the beginning, Muhammad had very few followers and funds. He was treated with much hostility. The first battle of Badr[40] was fought between Muhammad and his relatives. It was the first time that the powerful and rich Koresh government was defeated along with his nobles by a small band of soldiers. With this victory a new power had arisen in Arabia. The authority of the apostle, Muhammad, was strengthened in the region. Local Arab tribes began to convert and ally themselves with the Muslims and the expansion of Islam began.

Before the occurrence of the battle of Badr, Muhammad tried to avoid a direct confrontation with his relatives. The budding movement faced growing opposition and persecution. They were persecuted in so many ways that they had to hide or immigrate to other countries like Ethiopia. Muhammad commanded his followers to be tolerant. Some influential members of his family would laugh at and mock him. For instance, once when Muhammad was prostrated in prayer, they put very dirty things on his back and shoulders and ridiculed him[41].

There was no chance for the believers to win the battle of Badr. Their number was too small. The followers of Muhammad were not taken very seriously by the powerful army of Koresh[42]. Muhammad asked help from God and when it was granted he decided to engage in battle. God assisted him in the battle of Badr by sending a thousand angels. *"When you sought help from your Lord who told you: 'I will assist you with a thousand angels' [Koran 8.9]".* God had also given him the news that he will be victorious, but Muhammad was still not peaceful[43]. The main reason why the Lord wanted the battle was that He was not at all pleased with the behavior of Mecca's authorities who arranged the performance of various religious rites. The priests of Mecca were obstructing people from the Holy Mosque although they were not its appointed guardians [Koran 8:34]. They were receiving funds and spending it for their own personal maintenance and were turning men away from God [Koran 8:36]. They were the worst creatures, they denied the truth and they did not believe [Koran 8:55]. They were treacherous and they broke treaties [Koran 8:58]. Therefore, to replace them by a new administration, a battle was necessary.

The Mahābhārata[44] also describes the battle in the holy place of Kurukshetra[45] as a violent clash between family members. Prior to the battle of Kurukshetra Bhagavad-gītā was spoken by Lord Krishna to Arjuna. Because Dhritarashtra was blind, he was disqualified from ruling the kingdom. After the death of his brother, Pandu[46], his sons became the rightful heir to the throne. Dhritarashtra[47], who was Pandu's elder brother, wanted the kingdom for his one hundreds sons instead of the five sons of Pandu. His eldest son, Duryodhana, formed a conspiracy against the five sons of Pandu[48], so that he could rule the kingdom. Dhritarashtra knew that this was sinful, but because of his extreme attachment to his wicked son, Duryodhana, Dhritarashtra supported him. Dhritarashtra refused to accept all negotiations for peace by the Pandavas. The eldest brother of the Pandavas, Yudhiṣṭhira, was the rightful heir to throne. He was highly righteous and always thought of the citizens' welfare. By material calculation it was not possible for the Pandavas to win the battle against the vastly superior forces of Dhritarashtra's army. Duryodhana was extremely confident that his party would win the battle.

Before the Battle of Kurukshetra, every effort was made by the Pandavas to avoid the war, but the other party was determined to fight. According to the Vedic system, a giver of poison, one who sets fire to one's house, one who attacks others with deadly weapons, one who plunders riches, one who occupies another's land, and one who kidnaps one's wife, is fit to be punished, and no sin is incurred by punishing such an aggressor. All of these crimes were committed by Duryodhana against the Pandavas. Arjuna, the most intimate servant of the Lord, out of material sentiment, refused to fight with his own kinsmen. He thought it would be better to let them rule the kingdom rather than kill them.

Declining to fight

As Arjuna was unwilling to fight against his friends and relatives in the battle of Kurukshetra, a section of the followers of Muhammad were averse to participate in the first military expedition of the battle of Badr. Arjuna was famous as a warrior who had never been defeated. For him not to fight would have been a complete disgrace. Seeing their eminent death, Arjuna felt compassion for the soldiers of the other camp, many of whom were his intimate friends, relatives and teachers. He was thinking, how could he enjoy life, if all his family members were killed on the battlefield? He was afraid that, by killing them, he would become sinful. If the elders of the family were killed then there would be no one to guide the family in the proper execution of the scriptures. The harmony and prosperity of the family would be lost. Being confused about his duty, he became overwhelmed with despair[49]. Being so bewildered he decided to voluntarily surrender to Lord Krishna as a disciple so that he could remove his confusion[50]. *"Now I am confused about my duty and have lost all composure because of miserly weakness. In this condition I am asking You to tell me for certain what is best for me. Now I am Your disciple, and a soul surrendered unto You. Please instruct me [Bg.2:7]".* It is at this point of Arjuna's submission to Lord Krishna in the mood of disciple that Krishna's teaching of Bhagavad-gītā actually begins.

After embracing Islam, some of the followers of Muhammad declined to fight mainly because of fear of losing their lives, possessions and their loved ones. Also they were fearful of the austerities of the war such as lack of food, extreme heat in the desert, etc. and the fact that they were greatly outnumbered. The Koran labels them as hypocrites, because they did not help Muhammad in such a difficult time. The Koran describes their refusal as follows: One party refused to fight [Koran 3:121]. The number of the enemies' army was twice than that of Muhammad's [Koran 3:13]. They were enamored by earthly pleasures in the form of women, children, hoarded heaps of gold and silver, well bred horses, and tilled land and cattle [Koran 3:14]. They were reluctant to take part in the battle because they disliked fighting [Koran 2:216].

Arjuna and some of the followers of Muhammad were presented with a difficult task. They naturally felt uneasy and hesitated to execute it. Lacking decisiveness they became unable to act with full determination. Fear, weakness of heart, undue attachment related to the body and its relations, and speculation about the outcome of an issue weakens one's resolute sense of purpose. Influenced by doubts and fear one feels dejected and desires to abandon his duty. One's intelligence becomes clouded due to material illusion. Bewildered by greed one is blinded by excessive desire to enjoy the possessions of others. Because of excessive attachment to the bodily conception of life, one is disturbed by intense heat or cold in the course of one's duty and thinks of his material comfort.

In the battle of Kurukshetra Arjuna was so much afflicted with lamentation that he decided to abandon his duty to fight on the battlefield. Arjuna thought that his victory in the battle would only cause sorrow and grief for him. He envisioned painful reverses in the battlefield. He thought that he would not be happy even by gaining victory over the foe. Due to fear his whole body was trembling, his hairs were standing on end and his skin was burning[51]. H was faced with a bewildering situation. Confronted with such a dilemma, Arjuna presented few moral arguments. To dispel his confusion, he decided to take full shelter of the Supreme Lord's guidance.

Receiving supreme guidance

Arjuna refused to do his duty because he thought that the temporary bodily relationship with his kinsmen was more important than his relationship with God. He became bewildered. With every step in life there are perplexities. To overcome these perplexities, Arjuna took superior guidance from the Supreme Lord to give him the proper perspective for action. This indicates that Arjuna would soon be free from the false lamentation resulting from bodily affection. He would be enlightened with perfect spiritual knowledge, and would then surely do his duty as a warrior. This is the way to curb all lamentation for good, to take shelter in God. Since he would be enlightened by Krishna, soon, his dilemma will be removed.

Lord Krishna rebuked him for his misplaced compassion. The Lord told him that as the body is destined to die, compassion should be applied to the soul. The body is simply an outward dress *"The Supreme Personality of Godhead said: While speaking learned words, you are mourning for what is not worthy of grief. Those who are wise lament neither for the living nor for the dead [Bg.2.11]".* Compassion, lamentation and tears are all signs of ignoring the existence of the true spirit soul. Arjuna's lamentation for his kinsmen is certainly not befitting. He who knows what the body is and what the soul is does not grieve. Arjuna thought that religious principles based on material bodily relationship are more importance than the knowledge of distinguishing the body from the soul. His sorrow is due to a lack of knowledge. Because he was lacking in spiritual knowledge, he is not a very learned man. As he is not a very learned man, he was consequently lamenting for something which was unworthy of lamentation. The body is born and is destined to be vanquished soon or later. The body is not as important as the soul. One who knows this is actually learned. For him there is no cause for lamentation, regardless of any condition of the material circumstances. Compassion for the eternal soul leads to establish a relationship with God. Compassion for the dress of a drowning man is senseless. A man fallen in the ocean cannot be saved simply by rescuing his outward dress, the gross material body. One who does not know this and unnecessary grieves for the outward dress is not learned. To help Arjuna come to his senses, Krishna made an analytical description of the body and the soul. *"For the soul there is neither birth nor death at any time. He has not come into being, does not come into being, and will not come into being. He is unborn, eternal, ever-existing and primeval. He is not slain when the body is slain [Bg.2.20]"*. To become free from all false egoistic misconceptions, Arjuna has to do his duty with the fixed conviction that he is a spirit soul different from the material body. Doubts begin from the misconception of the material body, which is accepted as the self. Uncertainties due to misconceptions of "myself" and "mine", "my body," and "my community" cause bewilderment for the soul.

Arjuna should do his duty for the sake of duty without considering any selfish motivation. In success or no success, he has to always be steady in his determination. *"Do thou fight for the sake of fighting, without considering happiness or distress, loss or gain, victory or defeat—and by so doing you shall never incur sin [Bg.2.38]"*. In case he refuses to do his duty, the great generals who had come to fight will not think that Arjuna has left the battlefield out of compassion for his brothers, teacher and grandfather. They will think that he left out of fear for his life. Their high estimation of his personality will be lost. For a respectable person dishonor is worse than death. Arjuna's fear for the temporary bodily relationship does not lead to the heavenly planets but to infamy[52]. The Lord told him that: "*Either you will be killed on the battlefield and attain the heavenly planets, or you will conquer and enjoy the earthly kingdom. Therefore, get up with determination and fight [Bg.2.37]"*.

In the Koran some of the followers of Muhammad declined to fight mainly because of the fear to lose their lives. Arjuna also wanted to abandon his duty out of fear that his grandfather and teacher die in the battle. On the pretext of saving their life, he wanted to flee from the battle to save his own. It is not that every warrior has to meet death in the battlefield. Death may come even while comfortably sitting at home. *"Wherever one is, death will reach him. No one can be saved from death, even if he is in the midst of the mightiest tower building [Koran 4: 78]. No one can die before his appointed term [Koran 3:143]". "One who has taken his birth is sure to die [Bg.2.27]".* The objection of the believers is a symptom of ignoring the real self. The body is born and is destined to be vanquished today or tomorrow. The body is perishable, subject to disease and pain. A powerful king and a street impoverished dog, both, have to taste terrible death. The soul is imperishable, full of knowledge and joy. For one who knows this, there is no cause of grief. Duty should be executed in spite of material inconveniences.

The common force that drives everyone to serve in different ways is a search for higher standard of happiness. However, happiness cannot be achieved just by pampering the material body. Real happiness is an essential quality of the soul. A neglected captive bird cannot survive just by polishing its golden cage. "*The life of this world is nothing but comfort and illusion [Koran 3:185]. Know that your worldly possessions and children are just a temptation for you and with God is the greatest reward [Koran 8:28].* As happiness is not possible for a bird that is kept in a golden cage with sumptuous foodstuff, in the same way, no amount of materialistic bodily comfort can bring happiness to the soul. To realize that one is a spirit soul one has to work for God without attachment to the result of work. "*If God would have ordered them to sacrifice their lives or to leave their homes, very few of them would have done it. But if they had done it, it would have been best for them. They would have gone farthest to strengthen their faith [Koran 4:66].* The need of the spirit soul is to get out of the limited sphere of materialistic life and fulfill his desire for complete freedom. He wants to see the free light and the spirit. That complete freedom is achieved when one acts to please the Supreme Lord.

Muhammad left his house, family and possessions and went forth to deliver the revelation [Koran 8:5]. "*Whoever leaves his country in duty to God will find many places of refuge, and abundance on the earth [Koran 4: 100]*". In the past many prophets along with their followers pleased the Lord by taking shelter of Him in the midst of difficulty. When they met with disaster they never lost heart nor did they weaken [Koran 3:146]. "*In time of disaster they used to pray to God, 'O Lord, forgive our sins, absolve anything we may have done that transgressed our duty, steady our steps and help us against those that resist faith [Koran 3:147]'*". "*Being freed from attachment, fear and anger, being fully absorbed in Me and taking refuge in Me, many, many persons in the past became purified by knowledge of Me—and thus they all attained transcendental love for Me [Bg. 4.10]*".

The concept of holy war

Both the Vedic system and the Koran recommend fighting. However, at the present moment the Vedic literatures do not recommend holy war for the majority of people are immoral. In order to engage in a holy war, one must follow godly principles as a soldier. He has not to be motivated by false ego [Bg. 18:17]. At present it is very difficult to find a person with such character. It involves a higher state of true devotion to God.

Modern civilization is considered to be more advanced in sensual enjoyment. Formerly, the advanced condition was considered to be in righteousness. Man has flourished economically, so at present, he is not very interested in moral codes. Many places of worship are now practically not in use. Men are more interested in factories, shops, and cinemas than in a spiritual quest. Therefore, at present the Vedic system recommends that, rather than killing impious persons through a holy war, it is better to remove their tendency for ungodly acts through the recitation of the holy names of the Lord. Indeed, by reciting the names of the Lord, all bad qualities are gradually removed from the heart of the impious persons. One automatically develops divine qualities. Chaotic conditions in human society are either averted or reduced. Therefore, at the present, Vedic teachings do not at all recommend holy war.

According to the Vedic system, to participate in a holy war one has to be a warrior with the following qualities: *"Heroism, power, determination, and resourcefulness, courage in battle, generosity and leadership are the natural qualities of work for the warrior [Bg.18.43]".* A warrior is one who sacrifices his life to protect women, children and other weaker and innocent members of society. At present warriors are self interested, lacking in leadership qualities and often either involved in political clashes or collecting funds for their personal sense enjoyment. For instance, as a political leader, Stalin was responsible for a minimum of twenty million deaths resulting from the terror famine in the Ukraine, the purges, and the Gulag[53].

In a holy war, only those with the qualities of a warrior were involved in battle. No civilians were killed. Children, woman and elderly people were protected. At present the soldiers do not follow the chivalrous codes of religious conduct as prescribed in the Holy Scriptures. Many innocent women, children and elderly are cruelly tortured and killed in so-called holy wars. Although fascism and Nazism were uprooted during the Second World War, more civilians than combatants died. About twenty out of every one hundred homes in Germany were destroyed. Two and a quarter million homes were destroyed in Japan and 460,000 in Great Britain. Every fifth Greek was left homeless and 28,000 homes in Rotterdam, Holland, were obliterated. Tens of millions of people were uprooted from their homes during the war. At least five million people from eastern Germany and the Baltic states died from murder, starvation, and exposure after being expelled from their homes[54].

Therefore, a war should be avoided at any cost. War is always dangerous for it brings destruction and devastation. The Vedic literatures stress that one has to first show tolerance. Violence can be used only as a last resort. In the Vedic tradition there are four means to avoid war. If one observes the first three of these tactics and cannot find a peaceful solution then war becomes inevitable. These four means are: 1) sāma: pacification, or praising your opponent with pleasing words; 2) dāna: the giving of gifts, such as land, in the spirit of reconciliation; 3) bheda: an intimidating threat leading to a peaceful alternative; 4) danda: punishment or war, which is only engaged in if the prior three attempts had failed. The intelligence and character of a leader must be of a very high caliber in order to apply these positive alternatives to war.

In the Vedic system fighting is more understood as doing one's prescribed duty for the satisfaction of the Lord. Fighting for the Lord's cause does not only mean violent war. To peacefully act for the interest of the Supreme Lord is always considered the best course of action, except when fighting cannot be avoided for the sake of protecting the citizens. To act for the satisfaction of the Lord is the duty of everyone because every soul is originally a servant of the Supreme Lord.

At present, many people in the world think of Islam to be a fanatical and at times violent religious faith. In the past, the concept of jihad was preached by different Muslim factions or state leaders as a means to solve different political problems. How could Islam be appreciated as a religion of peace if the concept of holy war is accepted? The early history of Islam involves expansion through military conquest and civil wars. For almost three hundred years, various Islamic factions struggled for power. Assassinations, massacres, executions and inquisitions of Muslims by Muslims were common place.

Muhammad employed the use of military force because there was no other alternative to check this continual bloodshed and to bring unity and peace. After his death, his first four successors known as the rightly guided caliphs were involved in many wars. Abu Bakr[55], the prophet's close friend and early follower, found himself preoccupied with the wars of apostasy. Omar[56], another direct associate of the prophet, sought to preserve the unity of the Muslim community by extending the raids to neighboring countries. Othman[57], another associate of Muhammad, continued the raids. Ali's[58] rule was marred by five years of civil war. In this light, Islam may seem to be a religion that promotes violence rather than peace, but actually this is not the fact.

In Islam there is diversity of opinion regarding the meaning of the word 'jihad' or 'holy war'. Some Muslims promote the conquest of one's self as 'the greater holy war'. They express a negative opinion about violent religious conflict regarding it as 'the small holy war'. For them, the struggle with one's own soul is the greater struggle or the greater 'holy war'. The war against injustice, the disbelievers and oppressors is not the main struggle. The great jihad is the jihad against material desires and the evil residing within oneself. The jihad against material desires is much more difficult because it involves a person's struggle with his lower nature. The jihad against the unbelievers is not as difficult as struggling against one's lower nature.

In spite of strong arguments for the idea that the greater jihad is the jihad in pursuance of the pure self, some Muslims resist such a concept. They put forward the argument that fighting, or holy war, is applied to accomplish the ultimate goal of Islam; that to create a political Islamic state, there must be holy war. Though, in Islam there is diversity of opinion regarding the meaning of the word 'jihad', the ultimate point of all scriptures given by God is peace and harmony among all living beings. People of godly character never cause unnecessary suffering to anyone.

A gradual rise

Man wants God to help him achieve all success for selfish satisfaction. Knowing this enjoying mentality, the Koran and Vedic literatures give a process called fruitive activities. By following such process, man can satisfy his material desires and at the same time worship God. In this process, little interest is given to God. Yet, it is meant to gradually elevate the performer to a spiritual platform. Even though one has material desires, God is still given a singular position. A little endeavor to please the Lord is of great value. By acting both for oneself and God, one gradually comes to know the difference between matter and spirit. A slight amount of service to God purifies one. Moreover, the faith in the existence of the heavenly planets will soon bring one to desire the Kingdom of God.

As a high-minded soul, Arjuna was afraid that by fighting against his relatives for political reasons, he would be affected by sin. "*Alas, how strange it is that we are preparing to commit greatly sinful acts. Driven by the desire to enjoy royal happiness, we are intent on killing our own kinsmen [Bg. 1.44]*". "*Better for me if my relatives, weapons in hand, were to kill me unarmed and unresisting on the battlefield [Bg. 1.45]*". Fearing the reaction of sin, he taught that it would be better to forgive them on the ground of saintly behavior. He wanted to retire from active life and practice spirituality in a secluded place. He wanted to skillfully avoid the fighting by using spiritual life as an excuse. As a sincere student, he asked Krishna what is the best course of action? In answer, Krishna told him: *"If you do not perform your religious duty of fighting, then you will certainly incur sins for neglecting your duties [Bg.2.33]"*. Inaction is sinful. One has to perform his prescribed duty, for action is better than inaction. To encourage one who is not willing to perform his prescribed duties, the Koran and Vedic wisdom teach that it is better to perform one's duty with an enjoying spirit than be inactive. Of course, this is not the highest spiritual guidance. Using one's prescribed duties and using the teachings of Vedic literatures and the Koran for the purpose of one's personal enjoyment is not considered the highest instruction. Yet, it is better than inaction. To prevent inactivity, some portions of the scriptures emphasis material enjoyment in the name of religion. To inspire the believers and Arjuna to do their duty, rewards of the heavenly planetary sensual enjoyments are promised. In case death occurs in the battlefield, the heavenly enjoyment is promised. In case the battle is won, earthly enjoyment is gained. And by declining to act, one's existence is hellish. To not become sinful, Krishna told Arjuna that, as a householder warrior, he has to do his duty. In case he dies in the battlefield, he will be promoted to the heavenly planet to enjoy its celestial damsels. If he wins the battle, he can rule the earth. However, if he leaves the battlefield, dishonor will overtake him. He will enter the hellish planet. *"Happy are the warriors to whom such fighting opportunities come unsought, opening for them the doors of the heavenly planets [Bg.2.32]". "If, however, you do not perform your religious duty of fighting, then you will certainly incur sins for neglecting your duties and thus lose your reputation as a fighter [Bg.2.33]". "People will always speak of your infamy, and for a respectable person, dishonor is worse than death [Bg.2.34]". "Either you will be killed on the battlefield and attain the heavenly planets, or you will conquer and enjoy the earthly kingdom. Therefore, get up with determination and fight [Bg.2.37]". "The great generals who have highly esteemed your name and fame will think that you have left the battlefield out of fear only, and thus they will consider you insignificant [Bg.2.35]". "Your enemies will describe you in many unkind words and scorn your ability. What could be more painful for you? [Bg.2.36]"*

To encourage one to do his duty, the Koran as Vedic texts use similar approach. Either the believers have to be killed on the battlefield and attain the heavenly planets, or conquer the foe and enjoy the booty of the war. *"For one who fights in the cause of Allah, whether slain or victorious, I shall soon give him a great reward [Koran 4.74]". "If you are slain, or die, in the way of God, forgiveness and mercy from the Lord are far better than all they could amass [Koran 3:157]". "Who left their homes in the cause of the Lord, and are slain, on them the Lord will bestow a goodly provision [Koran 22.58]. He will admit them to a place with which they shall be well pleased [Koran 22.59]".* The Koran also stated that in case the believers win the battle they can enjoy the booty of the war. *"They will acquire many acquisitions, booty and gain which they will take [Koran 48.19]". "Whatever you take as spoils of war, a fifth is for God, the messenger, orphans and the needy [Koran 8.41]".*

To inspire one to his duty, indirect persuasions are included in the scriptures. For instance, to make a child take a bitter medicine, the father entices him by promising, 'take this medicine, and then you can have a nice sweat cake'. Such indirect persuasion conceals the actual purpose of the father. Since the great majority of people are addicted to sense gratification, the Koran and Vedic literatures offer an appealing program of sense enjoyment in the heavenly planets. In this way, the common men can control their senses for the path to God and sense pleasure goes ill together. Persons who are materialistically minded are very much attracted by these persuasions. To seduce or to originate fear, the Koran and the Vedic texts use reward and punishments to lure the ignorant.

Arjuna and the believers were not ready to just do their duty for the sake of duty. To inspire them to do their duty, in the Koran and Vedic texts, the process of fruitive activities is given. However, the ultimate instruction of the Koran and Vedic literatures is to give up all other engagements and fully surrender unto the Supreme Lord. In all Vedic texts and the Koran the worship of God is much stressed. One is gradually promoted to the understanding that one's actual self-interest is to surrender to God. As stated in the Manu-saṁhitā: "Although fruitive religious activities are very much popular among the conditioned souls, the actual perfection of life is achieved when one gives up all fruitive endeavors[59]." An intelligent person can immediately understand by direct analysis the actual purpose of Vedic literature and the Koran which ultimately aim at achieving God.

For the sake of duty

The Vedic and Koranic texts do not end in the irrelevant pleasures found in the earthly and the heavenly planets. To attract the mind of ordinary men, blessings are offered in the Koran and Vedic literatures. In this way, by developing little faith, there is an interest to study scriptures. By analyzing sacred texts, discrimination between the temporary and the eternal develops. One gradually becomes averse to temporary worldly things and hankers after God. A change of consciousness happens with selfless service to God.

Arjuna was still not convinced. He did not doubt that anyone killed in the battlefield will attain the heavenly planets and that when one conquers the enemy, he enjoys the earthly kingdom. Yet, he thought that, if he engages in a ghastly battle with the intention of getting a kingdom or with the desire to enjoy the heavenly facilities, still sin will overcome him.

To solve this dilemma, Krishna taught him higher knowledge of how to get free from sinful reactions. Arjuna has to execute his prescribed duty with a proper consciousness. Suffering the consequence of sin arise when duty is performed with a perverted materially contaminated consciousness. To avoid the consequence of sin arising from the battle, Krishna advices the following: *"Do thou fight for the sake of fighting, without considering happiness or distress, loss or gain, victory or defeat—and by so doing you shall never incur sin [Bg.2.38]". "Without being attached to the fruits of activities, act as a matter of duty, for by working without attachment one attains the Supreme [Bg.3.19]". "Surrendering all your works unto Me, with full knowledge of Me, without desires for profit, with no claims to proprietorship, and free from lethargy, fight [Bg.3.30]".*

Seeing how sincere and intelligent Arjuna is, Krishna is now giving him a higher Knowledge. He told him to do his duty without aspiring for a kingdom, heaven or hell. Duty has to be performed for the sake of the Lord. He, who acts for his own selfish sake, will be subject to the reaction of good or bad. He, who has completely surrendered himself to God, is free from any reaction. Arjuna has to do his duty without considering happiness or distress, loss or gain, victory or defeat [Bg.2.38]. He has to act for God without being attached to the fruits of his activities [Bg.3.19]. He has to surrender all his work unto God without desires for profit and with no claims to proprietorship [Bg.3.30]. As a spirit soul, different from the body, Arjuna has to be attached to God; rather, than be materially attached. Freedom from sinful reactions is possible by possessing the knowledge of how to work in detached way [Bg.2.39]. The realization of this knowledge is achieved while acting for God. This knowledge is revealed not by renouncing work, but by working for God. It is not the activity that should be renounced; rather, while working for the Lord, a consciousness of renunciation is needed. One has to do his duty with the knowledge that he is an eternal servant of the Supreme Lord. Without this knowledge, while acting, one will be subject to fear. If one acts for the sake of gaining a kingdom or the heavenly planets the mind will not be firmly fixed on the truth. One will be diverted by various types of fruitive acts. An unshakable resolution depends on the disposition of the mind. The state of mind of one who is engaged in securing heavenly enjoyment, sons, cattle and possessions are endless. Since the purpose is divided, the resolution will not be one. The disposition of the mind has to be marked with a single resolution and unshakable conviction. This is only possible when the mind is fixed on God. The purpose and the aim have to be one, not many-branched [Bg. 2.41]. To be free from the reaction of work, Arjuna has to develop the knowledge of how God is the real proprietor. Freedom from the bondage of actions is possible when one is doing everything for God without attraction for the results good or bad of his action. Any other action binds the worker. To get free from the bondage of action Krishna proposes the following: *"Abandoning all attachment to the results of his activities, ever satisfied and independent, he performs no fruitive action, although engaged in all kinds of undertakings [Bg.4.20]". "He gives up all sense of proprietorship over his possessions, and acts only for the bare necessities of life. Thus working, he is not affected by sinful reactions [Bg.4.21]".*

In the Koran, the believers are asked to act for God without any selfish concern. *"We ordered them to sacrifice their lives and leave their homes, but few could do it. If they have done it, it would have been best for them. They could have gone farthest to strengthen their faith [Koran 4.66]".* To strengthen one's faith in the revelation, the believer has to use their assets, time and actions in the service of God without being anxious about the outcome. Faith is attained by using one's possessions and time in glorifying God. Over and above this, one should control the senses. A person who controls the senses while serving God attains great faith in the Lord. Due to greed, covetousness, pride, arrogance and desire for sense gratification, one may again become faithless. In the Koran they are descriptions of how some believers were overcome by the reaction of work. At first they were guided, but they became again arrogant. The Lord has bestowed His bounty on some believers, but they become overconfident with their achievement [Koran 9.75]. The Lord made a covenant with them, that they would be charitable, full of love and generosity, and righteous [Koran 9.75]. But they were overcome with pride. They became covetous, broke their promises and adverse [Koran 9.76]. They were almost able to defeat the enemy, but when they saw the booty, which they covet, they fell in dispute and disobeyed the order [Koran 3.152]. You were climbing the high ground, without even casting a side glances at any one. The messenger called you back. There did the Lord give you one distress after another by way of requital, to teach you not to grieve for the booty that had escaped you and for the ill that had befallen you [Koran 3.153]. Because of their arrogance, the Lord put hypocrisy in their hearts [Koran 9.77]. Due to malicious behavior[60], hypocrisy[61], pride, disloyalty[62], ill talks about others, not seeking detachment, arrogance[63], disobedience [64] and lack of knowledge about God and the soul[65], their faith is lost. While making an external show of dedication, inwardly there is attraction to material subjects that are unrelated to God. They become deceitful. The main cause of losing faith is that a fruitive worker lacks a selfless meek service attitude towards God. Rather than following the Lord's guidance, one follows his material desires. One sinks under the weight of his accumulated sinful reactions.

The process of fruitive activities is not perfect. A mentality of duality in the form of happiness and distress, profit and gain, victory and defeat develops. To strengthen their faith further, the Lord asked the believers to sacrifice everything for His sake, but few could do it. If they have done it, it would have been best for them. They could have gone farthest to strengthen their faith [Koran 4.66]. What was said about the people of the book is also applicable to the believers: *"You will indeed find them most greedy for life; even more than the idolaters. Each one of them wishes He could live for thousand years. But the grant of such life will not save him from punishment [Koran 2.96]"*. Doubts, that cause great bewilderment for the soul, begin with the misconception of identifying the soul with a certain family, nation and community. With the full knowledge that every soul is originally a servant of the Supreme Lord, one has to surrender his work to God. By assimilating this important instruction, all misconceptions and illusions are at once mitigated. Faith and determination to consent to work for God is possible when the soul is equipped with spiritual wisdom. In such state of confidence, even in the midst of the greatest calamities, there is nothing to fear. The Lord will supply all intelligence, power and material necessities to his faithful servant.

Chapter Four
Motivated religion

Abraham was beyond religious affiliations

There was a quarrel between the Jews and the Christians as to whether Abraham was a Jew or Christian. The Jews claimed that he was Jew and the Christians claimed that he was a Christian. However, for God, Abraham's faith was more important than his belonging to a certain community. One may pretend to belong to a particular type of faith with reference to a particular religious sect, or a great religious leader, but it is one's faith and how sincerely one follows the instructions of the Lord that determines how much one is firmly convinced about the existence of God.

Most people are more interested in their nationality, community, society or particular political party, than in their spiritual relationship with God. From identification with one's community; sectarianism, favoritism, hate, pride, and quarrels arise. Consequently, one should be more concerned with the purpose of God's teachings, rather than to be anxious to advertise his religious affiliation. *"Do you say that Abraham, Ishmael, Isaac, Jacob and the Tribes were Jews or Christians [Koran 2:140]? Abraham was neither Jew nor Christian. He was true in faith. He bowed his will to Allah [Koran 3:67]".*

How was Abraham true in faith? His deeds were pleasing to God. The Lord does not consider one's caste, social position, color, community, nationality or religious affiliation. It is the purity of our motives in our thoughts and actions when dealing with others that satisfy Him. Abraham, Ishmael, Isaac and Jacob and their offspring had passed away. They achieved the ultimate success by pleasing the Lord with their actions. One who really loves them should follow in their footsteps. *"Those of mankind who have the best claim to Abraham are those who follow him [Koran 3:68]". "We make no distinction between Abraham, Ishmael, Isaac, Jacob, and the Tribes, and to God do we bow our will [Koran 3:84]." "Do you claim that Abraham, Ishmael, Isaac and Jacob and their offspring were Jews or Christians? Have you more knowledge than Allah? [Koran 2:140]'. 'They were people that had passed away. They shall reap the fruit of what they did, and you, of what you do. You will not be questioned about their deeds [Koran 2:141]".*

The purpose of the Vedic literature is to revive the eternal occupation of the living entity, sanātana dharma. It is the deeds in connection with the Lord that are pleasing to Him. To a person suffering from illness, it does not matter whether a doctor is Jew, Christian, or Muslim, if he has the qualification of a medical man. For the Lord, birth is not a consideration. If one's deeds are not meant for the ultimate cause, what is the use of being born as Jew, Christian or Muslim? If one falsely engages in frivolous temporary activities, will he be recognized by the Lord? There is no need to be very sophisticated in temporary engagement. All such grand temporary deeds, although perhaps very important for temporary life, have nothing to do with eternal life. Therefore, sanātana-dharma does not refer to any process of religion. It is the eternal function of the soul in relationship with the Supreme Lord. As liquidity cannot be taken from water, heat cannot be taken from fire. Similarly, the eternal function of the soul to please the Lord is inherent in every living entity. The constitutional position, of the soul is to render service to the Supreme Lord. *"It is the living-entity's constitutional position to be an eternal servant of Krishna [Cc Madhya 20.108]". "He said: 'I am indeed a servant of Allah. He has given me the revelation and He made me a prophet' [Koran 19:30]".*

In time, trees grow, branches develop, flowers blossom and fruits appear and then the tree dwindles and dies. Similarly, human beings are born, perform their different activities, reap the results and die. In the past, many great civilizations established prospering kingdoms and their accomplishments were vanquished in due course of time. However, many great saintly persons in the past exhibited wonderful godly character and their qualities and exemplary actions still inspire people today.

The collapse of past civilizations

Many wealthy and powerful civilizations were developed with great enthusiasm. They were very proud of their eminent position. Like a cloud passes in the sky, carried by the wind, so many so-called great civilizations have come and gone: The Egyptian, the Greek, the Roman, the Ottoman and the Mogul empires, etc., and in the modern day Hitler, Stalin, etc. By the waves of time, all that's left of them is a few archeological remains. *"How many generations that had far more wealth and pretension have God destroyed [Koran 19:74]? Can you find a single one of them or hear the last whisper of them [Koran 19:8]?"*

One historical example clearly given in the Koran is the great 'Ad[66] civilization. They constructed extraordinary monuments on every high hill but their effort was in vain [Koran 2:128]. They erected huge palaces thinking that they would live forever [Koran 26:129]. To them God sent the prophet Hud, who asked them, 'if you turn away, my Lord will put another people in your place [Koran 11:57]'. Worship God, [Koran 11:50], ask forgiveness from Him, and turn to Him in repentance [Koran 11:51]. *"They said: 'it is the same if you warn us or do not warn' [Koran 26:136], we shall not abandon our gods' [Koran 11:53]". These were the people of 'Ad, who denied the words of their Lord, rebelled against His apostles, and followed the bidding of every powerful and obstinate tyrant [Koran 11:59]. They were cursed in this life and they will be damned on the Day of Doom [Koran 11:60]. They rejected the prophet, Hud, and Allah destroyed them [Koran 26:139]".*

Vedic literature states that anything in relation with the body is impermanent. History shows that many powerful empires that were constructed with great pain and great perseverance were at once destroyed. *"Whatever is produced by the materialist with great pain and labor for so-called happiness, the Supreme Lord, as the time factor, destroys, and for this reason the conditioned soul laments [SB 3.30.2]".* The main function of the time factor is to destroy everything. The materialists are engaged in producing so many temporary things. They think that they will be happy by satisfying their material needs. They forget that everything that they have produced will be destroyed in due course of time. They think that by advancing in satisfying the material needs they will be happy, but they forget that everything they have produced will be destroyed in due course of time. *"What is with you will vanish and what is with Allah will endure [Koran 16.96]".*

From history we can see that there were many powerful empires on the surface of the globe that were constructed with great pain and great perseverance, but in due course of time they have all been destroyed. Still the foolish materialists cannot understand that they are simply wasting time in producing material necessities, which are destined to be vanquished in due course of time. This waste of energy is due to the ignorance of the mass of people, who do not know that they are eternal and that they have an eternal engagement towards God. They do not know that this span of life is but a flash of time. Not knowing this fact, they waste their time in creating more and more facilities for material enjoyment. *"The misguided materialist does not know that his very body is impermanent and that the attractions of home, land and wealth, which are in relationship to that body, are also temporary. Out of ignorance only, he thinks that everything is permanent [SB 3.30.4]". "O you, who believe, let not your riches and your children divert you from the remembrance of Allah [Koran 63:9]".*

A society based on the knowledge that one is spirit and related to God results in a thriving civilization with the highest quality of human culture. Animal culture means to solely satisfy the demands of the body. Human society is meant to develop a culture that satisfies the needs of the soul. Under material illusion grand civilizations collapsed due to a vacuum of spiritual values. A civilization detached from God is just like a separated hand or leg being detached from the whole body. No actual satisfaction is experienced by anyone. The leaders' attempts to bring about peace and prosperity, without putting God in the center, are illusory. Due to their attraction for material gain incompetent leaders are incapable of offering solutions. Finding solutions to the problems of this world lie in inquiring about how to achieve real happiness as a spirit soul in one's relationship with God.

The tendency to perform religious activities in exchange for material profit and utilize their earnings for worldly enjoyment is deeply rooted in men. The aim of religion, however, is to understand God with firm conviction. One has not, under the designation of being Jew, Christian and Muslim, to become proud. The highest aim of religion is to glorify God. One who loves other objects beside God cannot really exalt the Lord. *"There are some men who take for themselves objects of worship besides Allah, whom they love as they love Allah and those whose belief is overflowing in love for Allah [Koran 2.165]"*. Any object of worship beside the almighty God inflames and drives one madly on. Any self-seeking material gain troubles and weighs down the soul. If the Lord is the ultimate cause, one will be content with whatever comes. One should take care to not rely too much on any preconceived desire that has no reference to the Supreme Lord. *"The supreme occupation [dharma] for all humanity is that by which men can attain to loving devotional service unto the transcendent Lord. Such devotional service must be unmotivated and uninterrupted to completely satisfy the self [SB 1.2.6]". The occupational activities a man performs according to his own position are only so much useless labor if they do not provoke attraction for the message of the Personality of Godhead. Everyone is rendering some sort of service to others [SB 1.2.8]"*. There is a dormant affection for God within everyone. One has to engage in occupational engagements that awaken one's divine consciousness. The perfection of such activities is attained by transforming one's desires from I and mine centered to being God centered. One whose service is centered on God rejoices. He is free because he approaches God out of selfless love.

The path of desiring anything beside God is inferior. The path of those who have strong love for the Lord is superior. The actual goal to be realized in the name of religion is not the gain of sensual pleasure. The ultimate aim of religion is to reestablish one's bond with God in harmony with His will. The living entity is eternal, and his desires are also eternal. Desires cannot be stopped. With the development of the desire to attain God's kingdom, the desires for personal gain and honor will diminish in proportion to the development of one's desire to serve the Lord free from personal motivations.

Materially motivated religion

Man seeks God according to his state of mind. Some expects material reward from the Lord in the form of achievement of material gain. Others worship God to get relieve from material miseries in the form of sickness, poverty and death. *"When trouble touches a man, he cries unto Us. When We solve his trouble, he passes on his way as if he had never cried to Us [Koran 10:12]".* When a person is beyond material pain and gain, he engages in God's service without aspiring for any personal benefit. He naturally exalts God without motives of fear or desires to gain something. His only interest is to whole heartedly devote himself to God. To worship the Lord out of fear of material miseries or out of desire for material gain is not a pure level of worship. A person who takes to religious activities for material gain will never be able to understand God. Even a person who is not greedy for material possessions but attached to improving his material situation cannot deeply appreciate the Lord. Only the worship out of genuinc attraction is a rcal worship.

To free oneself from all fear, one should accept God with great faith as the supreme and surrender unto Him. God should be feared, instead of fearing loss or gain in the form of temporary material assets. *"Whosoever follows My guidance, he shall neither fear, nor grieve*

[Koran 2:38]". "Whoever submits his whole self to Allah and is a doer of good, he will get his reward with his Lord. He shall neither fear, nor grieve [Koran 2:112]". "Abandon all varieties of religion and just surrender unto Me. I shall deliver you from all sinful reactions. Do not fear [Bg.18.66]". One has to follow God's instructions without being concerned with motivated religious duties. Fear should be replaced with a sense of attraction for God. Trust in God vanquishes all fear and gain. Fear and material desire are extremely base. All different religion of the world calls man to renounce their material attachments. One has to withdraw from the world, but at the same time encounter the world by putting God in the center. Since everything belongs to God, all resources should be used in His service, in selfless surrender without material desire. Freedom from material attachment is incomplete without the surrendering unto Him. The difficulty that arise from renouncing worldly ties is resolved not by rejecting the world but by understanding the soul's relationship with God. When attraction for God appears by a systematic practice, all fears and all materially motivated religious thoughts disappear from the heart. Spiritual attainment grants eternity. Spiritual culture is infinitely better than a life motivated by materialistic values.

In Vedic literature and the Koran, blessings of material gain in the form of promotion to the heavenly planets and other benedictions are offered. Most people are attracted by such blessings as result of their religious performances. Too often religiosity is wrongly directed towards the fulfillment of desires rather than for the actual satisfaction of the Lord. It is stated in Vedic scripture that those who are captivated by the superior sensual pleasures available in the heavenly planets approach different gods[67]. To achieve excess pleasures, a person worships gods. Such a person does not achieve the actual goal of religion, which is becoming free from material desires in one's relationship with God. The Lord helps a sincere servant to give up his material attachment and completely surrender unto Him. Because the Lord does not give blessings of material opulence people neglect the Supreme Lord.

The lure of heavenly enjoyment

People desire to be promoted to the heavenly planets because they have no information about the Supreme Lord and His eternal kingdom. Although many scriptures mention the Lord and His abode, due to material desires, the soul's understanding about God is obscured. Clouded, the intelligence has less power to receive real knowledge about the Lord. As clouds darken the sky and obscure the bright sun from shining; as a dusty mirror cannot reflect a clear image; and as muddy water cannot reflect the visage of one that looks at it, material desires cloud the memory, mind and intelligence.

A soul that is guided by material desire becomes blind. Of little use are the eyes to a moth, since desire for the beauty of the light dazzles it and leads it into the flame. Material desires obscure the soul's understanding about God so that it cannot see the glories of the Supreme Lord. When light is set before the eye, the visual faculty is attracted by that which is interposed, it does not see other objects. Similarly, the dazzling light of heavenly enjoyment is so great that the believer totally ignores his worshipable Lord. In one's extravagant insanity, one is fully convinced that their spiritual journey ends with heavenly enjoyment.

Material desires deprive the soul of the mercy of God. There is less determination to achieve Him. The self is distinguished from matter; the soul is spiritual in constitution. It can never be fully satisfied by any amount of material enterprises. Although one desires a permanent secure and happy position, it is not possible. Any material desire that is not meant for God will eventually exhaust and fatigue the soul. Material desires are like restless and discontented children who are never satisfied. To attain that which is desired, so many endeavors are needed. Once that which is desired is attained, the soul is still weary, for it is never satisfied. *"Who is more astray than he who follows his lust without guidance from Allah [Koran 28:50]"?* "*The Supreme Personality of Godhead said: It is lust only, Arjuna, which is born of contact with the material mode of passion and later transformed into wrath, and which is the all devouring sinful enemy of this world [Bg. 3.37]"*. As an eternal soul, one's real happiness lies in the awakening of his relationship in servitude with the Lord. The more one serves the Lord, the happier he becomes, and this happiness increases without limit.

The Koran and the Vedic literature state that the eternal happiness which the soul wants is obtainable in the Kingdom of God. "*Allah has promised to men and women who believe gardens with streams of running water where they will abide forever and beautiful mansions in gardens of everlasting bliss. But the greatest bliss is the good pleasure of Allah: that is the supreme felicity [Koran 9:72]". "The thoughts of My pure devotees dwell in Me, their lives are fully devoted to My service, and they derive great satisfaction and bliss from always enlightening one another and conversing about Me. [Bg.10.9]"*

Arjuna sought guidance from Lord Krishna. That was the correct course of action for peace and harmony in the midst of his perplexities. Confused about his duty, Arjuna could find no means to drive away his grief. If material comforts could have driven away his lamentations, then Arjuna would not have said that even sovereignty like that of the gods in heaven could not dispel his lamentation. "*I can find no means to drive away this grief which is drying up my senses. I will not be able to dispel it even if I win a prosperous, unrivaled kingdom on earth with sovereignty like that of the demigods in heaven [Bg.2.8]".*

Even the pious gods who dwell in the heavenly planets have fallen short of the eternal kingdom of God. *"The gods have no power to relieve or to avert your distress. Those, whom they invoke, themselves seek the way to their Lord. Which one of them shall be the nearest? They hope for His grace and fear His chastisement [Koran 17:56-57]".* The Lord is eternal; therefore our relationship in servitude with Him cannot be destroyed, it is eternal. The gods also have an eternal relationship with God. They are seeking the way of their Lord. No soul has an eternal relationship with the gods. The gods are under the sway of death. *"They do not own power over their death or their life, nor can they be raised to life again [Koran 25:3]".*

People pray to be promoted to the heavenly planets because they have no knowledge about the opulence of the Supreme Lord. The Lord's magnificence is trillions and millions of times greater than the irrelevant opulence in the heavenly planets. Misguided and blinded by their material desires, the heavenly worshippers do not know how to reach the Supreme Lord. *"Men of small intelligence worship the demigods, and their fruits are limited and temporary. Those who worship the demigods go to the planets of the demigods, but My devotees ultimately reach My supreme planet [Bg.7:23]". "They have taken other gods apart from Allah that they might give them power and glory [Koran 19:81]".*

The kingdom of God is eternal and the heavenly planets are temporary. At the time of the destruction there will be no sun, moon and heavens. *"The sun and moon will be joined together [Koran 75:9]". "When the heavens is split asunder, [Koran 84:1]"* In the beginning of the creation there was only God. There was no sun, no moon, no water, no fire and no stars in the sky (Mahā Upaniṣad 1). Beyond the heavenly planet is the kingdom of God: *"His Throne does extend over the heavens and the earth [Koran 2:255]".* The earth, the sun, the moon and the heaven will eventually come to an end, but the kingdom of God is not affected because it is above the heaven and the earth. The Lord is the creator, maintainer and annihilator of everything. The creation exists by His will. Before the creation the Lord was there in His spiritual abode, and after the annihilation He will continue to remain. The Lord must exist before the creation, otherwise how could He be its Lord? If someone constructs a big building, this indicates that he must have existed before the building was constructed. God is not, one of the created beings. He is transcendental. It is He, God, who existed before the creation, it is He only who maintains the creation, and it is He only who remains after the annihilation of the creation. The spiritual planets of the Kingdom of God are all of a different nature. Their nature is not subjected to the rules of the material creation and annihilation. The existence of God implies the existence of His Kingdom, as the existence of a king implies the existence of his empire. *"Exalted be Allah, the True King! [Koran 20:115]".* The kingdom of Godhead is not void. It is full of spiritual varieties with great opulence of wealth and prosperity.

Moreover, if the gods and their heavenly planets are eternal, the delight of the heaven would equal that of the kingdom of God. Then, the gods along with the heavenly pleasure would either be equal or superior to the Lord. If the heavenly planets are eternal why would the gods be subject to death? There is no difference between one, who desires the sensuality of the heavenly planets, and one who worships directly a particular god. They are both foolish, for they have no desire to establish a permanent relationship in servitude with the Supreme God. In both cases they are deluded. A consciousness of duality in the form of desire and hate is not dissipated from their impure mind. They continue to be distracted by material desires, falling short of the Kingdom of God.

Material desires delude one's consciousness. One is unable to deeply understand his relationship with God. Being liberal, Vedic literatures do recommend worship of the gods in some places for the gradual upliftment of those who are still too materially attached. "*Men in this world desire success in fruitive activities, and therefore they worship gods. Quickly, of course, men get results from fruitive work in this world [Bg.4:12]"*. The Koran allows one to desire the heavenly planets that one can enjoy after death. Likewise, Vedic scriptures recommend the worship of different gods for one who desires to enjoy a particular benefit either in this life or the next: A diseased man can worship the sun god to achieve good health. One who desires elaborate sensual enjoyment can worship the moon god. One who desires to be very powerful can worship the god of fire[68]. There is no need to worship any god for one who is situated in the knowledge that he is the eternal servant of the Lord. Such persons are recommended to worship the Supreme Personality of Godhead alone[69].

While the Vedic system recommends the worship of the gods for one who is too materially attached, they do not encourage it. In Vedic literatures a detailed description is given about the worship of the gods, but the ultimate conclusion of Vedic teaching does not support the pantheism and the polytheism that pervades modern Hinduism. The many gods of the Hindu pantheon and the living entities are relegated to the status of subordinate servitors to the Supreme Lord.

Concocted worship

According to the dictionary idolatry refers to the worship of images that are not God. It is concocted worship by the imagination of the worshipper. Such worship is not prescribed in bona fide scriptures coming from God and His messenger. Even worshipping a person who is not worthy of such worship is not prescribed in scriptures.

Historically, during Noah's time, statues of great righteous leaders were erected after their death. Foolish people then began worshipping their statues though they were not worthy. Later generations did not even know why these statues had originally been erected. They only knew that their parents worshipped them to attain material benefits and they continued it. That is how idol worship started among Noah's people[70].

The first prophet who preached against idolatry was Noah, who was born thousands years after Adam[71]. Worship of the gods as described in the Vedic injunction is not considered sinful, although the Vedic system does not encourage it. However, any form of worship which is not prescribed by the scriptures is sinful. The rules and regulations of how to worship the gods are extensively explained in different Vedic literatures. A vivid example of idol worship that was not prescribed by the scriptures is the Jew's worship of the golden calf in a state of drunken, adulterous revelry. When Moses ascended Mount Sinai to receive the Lord's direction, in his absence, they molded an image of a golden calf and started its worship. *"Moses came unto you with clear proofs (of Allah's Sovereignty), yet, while he was away, you chose the calf (for worship) and you were wrongdoers [Koran 2:92]".* The worship of the calf that was performed was neither prescribed by God nor Moses, his messenger; therefore, it was completely sinful. Both God and Moses were, thus, very angry with their rebellious attitude.

At first Abraham was also a worshipper of the sun and the moon, later, however, he got a change of heart, he believed in one Supreme Lord. His humility, kindness and good character attracted the mercy of the Lord. As the people of Noah introduced unauthorized worship, so did Abraham's people. For instance, people in darkness worship dead spirits, the tombs of dead men and ghosts. Those who are not very conversant with the scriptural injunctions concoct different forms of worship. The people of Noah worshipped great righteous leaders as God. Similarly Abraham's people introduced new worship. Abraham smashes all their imaginative unauthorized deity forms into pieces. *"Abraham said to his father and his people, 'What are these images, to which you are devoted?' They said, 'We found our fathers worshipping them.' He said, 'Indeed you and your fathers have been in manifest error.'[Koran 21:52-54]". "Abraham broke all of them to pieces except the chief of them [Koran 21:58]". They inquired, 'Did you do this to our gods, O Abraham' [Koran 21:62]? 'No', he said. 'It was done by that chief of theirs. Ask them in case they can speak' [Koran 21:63]. They said, 'truly, as you know they cannot speak' [Koran 21:65]. He said, 'then why do you worship something apart from God that cannot profit you or harm you' [Koran 21:66]? They said, 'Burn him, and save our gods' [Koran 21:68]. Allah said, 'Turn cold, O fire, and saved Abraham' [Koran 21:69].*

These different kinds of worship are not actually God worship. God worship is for persons who base their worship on scriptural injunctions. As stated in the Koran: "*They devised names without authority from Allah and worshipped them [Koran 7:71]"*. Here the words *'without authority from God'* are very significant. According to the Vedic system, the worship of the gods is not considered idol worship if it takes into account that God is the Supreme Master of the gods. The worship of the gods is unauthorized if it does not consider the subordinate position of the gods in relationship to the Lord and if it does not follow the regulations given in the Vedic texts. Yet, the Vedic injunction does prescribe it for the gradual elevation of the foolish who cannot understand the supreme position of God and the subordinate position of all other living beings including the gods. Though the Vedic system do not recommend the worship of the gods, they do allow it and prescribe the process of how to do it properly, for it is better to worship the gods to satisfy one's material desires than to not follow any religious principles. All the gods are very much aware that any worship offered to them is actually for their supreme master, the Supreme Lord. The worshipper, who is too materially motivated, may not understand this. No god claims that he is the supreme God. Blinded by material desires, the common man neglects the Lord, and erroneously claims that the gods are as powerful as God.

An offence to the Lord's devoted servants, the gods, is taken very seriously by the Lord. "*Anyone who is an enemy to either God, or to His messengers and to His angels such as Gabriel and Michael, is certainly God's enemy [Koran 2:98]"*. Not just God should be given all respect and reverence, but also His servants. To blaspheme, offend or be envious toward the servant of God is a direct offence to the master. One who understands the position of the gods as servants of God neither blasphemes nor offends them in anyway. Rather, one offers them all respect as dear servants of the Lord. *"Those whom you call upon besides God are servants like you [Koran 7:194]"*.

The Vedic system does not recommend one to ask benedictions from the gods. But one who asks a favor from them is thousand times better situated than one who blasphemes them. A person may be wrong in approaching a king for some selfish material gain. But he is better situated than one who blasphemes him. For the offender may have his head chopped off by the king. If a human being in the position of a king can finish such a fool with one stroke of his sword, then what to speak of the celestial gods who are millions of time more powerful than earthly kings?

Muhammad and his followers completely abolished the system of the worship of the gods. This worship had degraded into rituals of drunkenness and adultery. This is described in the Koran. The priests of Mecca were obstructing people from the Holy Mosque although they were not its appointed guardians [Koran 8:34]. They were receiving funds and spending it for their own personal maintenance and were turning men away from God [Koran 8:36]. They were the worst creatures, they denied the truth and they did not believe [Koran 8:55]. They were treacherous and they broke treaties [Koran 8:58]. The priests were using the temple donations to buy wine, drugs and have all kind of illegal sexual enjoyment. An irresponsible life of degraded sexual enjoyment is not helpful to create good citizens for spiritual realization. Without a fixed wife, a priest who indulges in wine and gambling becomes a debauchee of the first order and is considered to be the greatest nuisance in society. In India, the system of worship of the gods is not degraded as it was in the time of Muhammad. The priests are following the Vedic injunctions. Such priests are neither drunk, nor engaged in sinful adulterous relationship. They have a higher standard of worship and cleanliness. Therefore, there was no need to abolish this system in India for this may help the foolish to become wiser. Most of these priests know that the Supreme Personality of Godhead is the chief living entity who is above all gods. The Vedic literature says that the clouds are controlled by the god of wind, heat is distributed by the sun-god, the soothing moonlight is distributed by the moon god, and the air is blowing under the arrangement of the god of air: "*It is because of My supremacy that the wind blows, out of fear of Me; the sun shines out of fear of Me, and the lord of the clouds, Indra, sends forth showers out of fear of Me. Fire burns out of fear of Me, and death goes about taking its toll out of fear of Me (*SB 3.25.42)*."*

In the lower stages of consciousness, there is a strong desire to satisfy the senses. Driven by such mentality, people may perform pious activities or religious rituals in order to gain something material. Actual attainment of religious activities culminates in the exclusive worship of the Supreme Lord. One who is full of material desire aims to gratify his own senses, while, a devoted servant aims to satisfy the Lord. Heavenly enjoyment is by far inferior to the service of the Lord. Service to God is eternal and joyful, unless it becomes polluted when mixed with the desire to satisfy the senses.

Beyond good work

It is very difficult to understand that even good work deepens one's material entanglement. Generally, one thinks that only sinful work has a harmful result. However, good work done with the mentality that 'I am the enjoyer of the fruit of my work' keeps one from realizing that he is not the doer, the Lord is. For instance, when Muhammad threw a small amount of dust during the battle of Badr causing difficulty to the other party, God chastised him by telling him: *"It was not you who killed them, but Allah did so. You did not throw the sand in the eyes of the enemies in the Battle of Badr, but it was I who did it [Koran 8:17]".*

Muhammad wrongly thought himself to be the doer of action. He was forgetful about the fact that it is God who is the ultimate director of all our activities, the supreme sanctioner. *"Not a leaf falls without His knowledge [Koran 6:59]". "It is out of the fear of the Supreme Lord that the wind is blowing* (*Taittirīya Upaniṣad* 2.8.1)*". "By the supreme order, under the superintendence of the Supreme Lord, the moon, the sun, and the other great planets are moving* (*Bṛhadāraṇyaka Upaniṣad* (3.8.9)). Mohammad thought himself to be the doer of action, but he did not consider the supreme sanction. One who knows that he is just an instrument of work and the Supreme Lord is the supreme sanctioner is perfect in doing everything. Such a person is never in illusion. Muhammad was empowered to achieve extraordinary task. This does not mean that it is due to his personal strength and power. The foolish thinks that whatever is happening is due to his personal, strength, knowledge and abilities. The Lord is all-powerful, and by His grace He can endow His servant with unlimited power. And when the Lord withdraws His power from anyone, that person becomes powerless. One should not be overconfident by possessing few borrowed plumes. All power is derived from God, the source of all power. Supremacy lasts as long as God desires. It ceases to act as soon as the Supreme Lord withdraws it. Just as all electrical power is received from the powerhouse by an expert engineer. As soon as the engineer stops supplying power, the bulbs are of no use. Similarly, in a moment's time power can be generated or withdrawn by the supreme will of the Lord. One has to remember to whom the power belongs? Instead of becoming puffed up by the false prestige of thinking himself the doer, he should desire to remain in his actual position as an instrument of the Lord. All the credit for any wonderful accomplishment must go to God. By such behavior only can one be free from the contamination of material affection and receive the benedictions of the Lord.

One should neither exult, nor be overjoyed, and presumptuous about his achievement. Rather one has to be humble and thankful for receiving God's help. The Lord assesses the dedication with which a man acts, rather; than the deed itself. He does much, who is dedicated. He does best, who serves God, rather than his own interests. That which seems service to God is often mixed with our self interest. One's own motives and inclination are seldom absent. On the contrary, a true servant seeks no self interest. He does everything for the glory of the Lord. He does not wish to rejoice in himself; rather he desires the greater glory of God above all things. He accepts no credit for himself, rather, attributes it wholly to God. He serves the Lord with a pure and straightforward purpose.

Lord Krishna also told Arjuna to be an instrument in the fight [Bg.11:33]. He who does God's will and renounces his own is truly a believer. He, who conforms entirely his desires according to the good pleasure of God, is an earnest doer of God's will. Material desires very often agitate one. One should be introspective and consider whether he acts for God's honor, or for his own personal advantage. If one acts for the pleasure of God, one will be satisfied with whatever He ordains. If, on the other hand, there is any self-seeking, one will be troubled and the weight of that hankering will pull him down. It is how sincerely one follows the instructions of the Lord that determines how much one is firmly convinced about the existence of God. One will be guided at every step of his life. Such person will ultimately attain the supreme destination.

Chapter Five
The ultimate Quest

A major test

As the Lord blessed Arjuna with knowledge of detachment similarly Abraham received such knowledge of the soul. This knowledge was able to free Abraham and his family from the misconception that arises from attachment to belonging to a certain family, a religion or nation. As Arjuna was asked to fight against, his relatives, Abraham in a dream was asked to slaughter his son Ishmael [Koran 37:102]. It was a big test for Abraham, who in his old age had longed for a son for such a long time. Being wise, compassionate and kind [Koran 11:75], Abraham spoke to his son about his vision. Ishmael encouraged his father to fulfill God's order. Here, one may take note that Abraham also tested his son. He did not force or plot to kill him. Ishmael was ready to fulfill the instruction of his father. Satan appeared before Abraham and Ishmael to try to deceive them. He was not as successful as he was with Adam, who transgressed. As a response, Abraham and Ishmael threw stones at him. Disappointed, Satan went to Abraham's wife, Hagar, the mother of Ishmael. When Satan told her that Abraham intended on slaughtering their only son, she did not believe him at first. But when she was told that Abraham was carrying out God's will, Hagar said: 'If it is God's will, let it be done'.

It is amazing that in this situation the mother, the father and the son all agreed to the proposal of God. Generally, ladies are very attached to their offspring, this is very natural. But Hagar showed the highest advancement in spiritual realization by overcoming Satan's attempt to deviate her from executing the Lord's will. Usually, when Satan comes between people, he is sure to harm at least one of them, but he was thwarted in his attempt even with the mother. Abraham, Ishmael and Hagar were beyond any mundane familial or communal attachment. They were rendering unalloyed service to God. Pure service to God is defined in Vedic literature as follow: One should be free from all material designations and cleansed of all material contamination. One should be restored to his pure identity as a spirit soul, in which he engages his senses in the service of the Lord who is the owner of the senses. That is called pure service to God [Nārada-pañcarātra]. *"Say, 'my worship, my service, my sacrifice and my living and my dying are for Allah, the cherisher of the worlds [Koran 6:162]".*

There are innumerable varieties of false designations that cover and create illusion in the soul. But Abraham, Ishmael and Hagar were not troubled by these artificial identifications related to the body, society and community. They were able to transcend them. This confirms their elevation to the highest standard of spiritual identity. Having established their relationship with God, they thought that their relationship with God is more significant than their bodily relationship. They did not hesitate to follow God's guidance. To develop a universal affection, not only for Ishmael, but for other beings, the Lord tested Abraham. In material consciousness, one's love is limited. But in spiritual consciousness, one develops a universal affection for all beings. One sees that everyone is eternally related to God.

Eternality in spirituality

The need to seek out God lies within all living beings. Unfortunately, most people of this world are so distracted with worldly pursuits that this primary need is generally never given top priority. Too often, it is ignored altogether. For one who is too busy with worldly pursuits, it is difficult to understand the Supreme Lord. Genuine inquiry to understand God is beyond fruitive activities, for the sole aim is no longer the achievement of earthly and heavenly happiness. To understand the Lord, one has to first know the difference between matter and spirit.

The difference between matter and spirit is that by nature, the body is ever changing, and the soul is eternal. *"Allah, the eternal, the absolute; He begets not, nor is He begotten [Koran 112:2-3]."* Allah, the Supreme Soul, exists permanently, remaining the same. The soul does not at any time become old, as the material body does. The changes of the material body do not affect the soul. The soul does not deteriorate like the body. The soul does not disintegrate like a tree, or anything material. *"For the soul there is neither birth nor death at any time. He has not come into being, does not come into being, and will not come into being. He is unborn, eternal, ever-existing and primeval. He is not slain when the body is slain [Bg.2. 20] [Kaṭha Upaniṣhad (1.2.18)]"*. The soul has no by-product either. The by-products of the body, children, are also different individual eternal souls. The body develops because of the soul's presence, but the soul does not change. The soul is free from the six changes: the body is born, it grows, it stays, it produces by-products, then it begins to decay, and at the last stage it vanishes. Therefore, Allah, He begets not, nor is He begotten. The Vedic system shares similar teaching as are stated in the Koran: *"That which pervades the entire body you should know to be indestructible. No one is able to destroy that imperishable soul. The material body of the indestructible, immeasurable and eternal living entity is sure to come to an end [Bg.2.17-18]"*. *"Allah, there is no god but Him: the living, the self-subsisting and the eternal. Neither slumber nor sleep overtakes Him [Koran 2:255]"*. *"Put your trust in Him, the one who lives and dies not [Koran 25:58]"*. Neither the Supreme Lord nor the spirit souls were ever born. The soul is unborn, eternal, ever-existing, and primeval. Such words as birth and death refer only to the external material body. The spirit soul is different from the external material body and resides in it like a passenger. *"At the moment of birth the spirit soul enters a material body and at the moment of death the soul leaves the body*

[Bṛhad-āraṇyaka Upaniṣhad 4.3.8]." *"The soul resides in the material body, when the body dies the soul does not die [Chāndogya Upaniṣad 6.11.3]."*

The material body will eventually be reduced to dust, but the soul is eternal. The Koran raises the question; *"When we are reduced to bones and dust, shall we really be raised up to a new creation [Koran 17:49]?"* After the death of the material body will one be again raised to life? Creation takes place through the combination of matter and spirit. The spirit soul is not created at any stage of material development. A child grows gradually to boyhood and then to manhood because of the presence of the soul. A dead child does not grow because the spirit is not present. The spirit souls are not inert dull matter, but they are living conscious beings. The soul, which is the vital force, is never born or created. It exists eternally. It has neither birth dates nor death dates. The saying that *'Allah, He begets not, nor is He begotten'* is correct, for the spirit soul is never born. In this way the scriptural description of the eternity of the soul is a factual truth.

Beyond the contaminated mind

The material body is the vehicle which is used to execute a variety of actions. The self, however, is not affected by all these bodily actions and subsequent reactions. Due to its subtle nature the soul never mixes with the material body. *"The sky, due to its subtle nature, does not mix with anything, although it is all-pervading. Similarly, the soul, being spiritual, although it is in the body, does not mix with the body [Bg. 13.33]."* By passing over a filthy place, air acquires the quality of that filthy place. The air and sunshine, which are spread everywhere, come in contact with both filthy places and sanctified places. However, the air and the sunshine are uncontaminated. The sunshine is aloof from all filthy things or sanctified places. Similarly, whilst in a material body, the soul seems to acquire different good or bad qualities, though the soul is pure. In fact it is the senses and the mind that becomes contaminated. The soul suffers or enjoys the actions and reactions of his past activities.

When the soul is dovetailed to the will of the Lord, one's suffering stops. For one who acts for the sake of God, there is no consideration of happiness or distress, profit or loss, victory or defeat. He, who acts, for his own senses, either in goodness or in passion, is subject to the reaction, good or bad. There is no reaction to material activities for one who has completely surrendered himself to God. If one can understand what sort of activities he should adopt, then all the actions and reactions of his past activities can be changed.

One suffers or enjoys by identifying himself with the body. However, the soul is beyond all bodily activities. For instance, Adam enjoyed great delight in the garden. Yet, by approaching the tree, he got into great distress. The Lord asked Adam to not approach the tree otherwise he will run into transgression. By approaching the tree, Adam sowed the seeds for his own suffering. The cause of the distress is forgetfulness of one's relationship with God. The cause of happiness is to know God to be the supreme. Every living entity is intended to abide by the dictation of God. When the mind is misled, one becomes entangled. For instance, one thinks that he can be happy if he has a very nice car. When the car is smashed in a collision, the mind suffers, and through the mind one suffers. Therefore, Adam's distress and happiness is due to his mind not to his soul. It is the mind that creates all these different conditioning.

The mind is connected to the material senses. So, ones state of mind manifests through the body and senses. For example if one has anger in the mind it is expressed through the tongue by vibrating many maledictions, through the hand by fighting, through the leg by kicking. Lust in the mind is expressed through lustfully glancing at a young woman. A mind infected by lust will think and speak about sexual affairs. Greed in the mind is expressed by securing money through illicit means. Fear in the mind is expressed through fear of death. Similarly, other mental states such as pride, lamentation and illusion are reflected by the actions of the material body. Absorption of the mind in different thoughts naturally subjects various transformations that are due to lust, anger, pride, greed, lamentation, illusion and fear. In this way, one identifies his body as the self. Absorbed in material activities and under the influence of false ego, he accepts the covering of different designations. Although one is a spirit soul, on account of his contact with material conditions, he is bewildered.

When Adam was acting under the direction of the Lord, he was free from any good or bad reactions. Satan could not harm him, for he never thought that he is the proprietor of action. His action of touching the tree was independent. It was faulty, because it was not pleasing the Lord. Adam was advised to act according to the direction of the Lord. To satisfy his own senses, Adam disobeyed the order of the Lord and ran into ruination; he lost his peace of mind. As long as one acts on his own account, he is subject to happiness and distress. If one does everything for the pleasure of the Lord without claim over proprietorship of his activities, one's action is not faulty. False sense of proprietorship is avoided by strict abidance of the order of Lord. Adam disobeyed, thus the entire responsibility of action was upon him. Adam's soul is by nature transcendental to all dualities, but because of his faulty mentality, he had to leave the garden. The spirit soul is beyond material existence, but, because of his perverted mentality as the enjoyer and false proprietor, one causes their conditioned life. Due to different mental conditions, one is put into advantageous and disadvantageous situations. The real benefit that can be brought to the suffering people is to change their faulty mentality. One should cooperate with the Lord without claiming false proprietorship over anything.

By absorption of the mind in a specific thought, a particular consciousness is acquired. As air is originally pure, however, in contact with a rose flavor, air acquires the quality of rose flavor. Similarly one's present day activities determine how he will think and act in the future. As a result of his disobedience to God, Adam's mind was not in correct order. Adam and Eve became aware of the fact that they were naked. Shame became manifest to them. Adam sought private benefits for himself and lost the garden. As a result of their breaking God's law, the couple was expelled from the garden and both received a curse. *"Allah said, 'get down with enmity to each other. On earth will be your dwelling place and your means of livelihood for a while [Koran7:24]".* The punishment given by the Lord to reside on earth is temporary. As soon as the soul voluntarily agrees to abide by the order of the Lord he is forgiven. He can return with the Lord as His eternal servant.

Freedom from material conditioning is possible by the regulation of the senses, and by serving the Lord. It is very difficult to control the mind and the senses without constantly remembering God. Without engaging the mind in the service of God, mundane thoughts cannot be stopped: *"Who remembers Allah while standing, sitting and lying on their sides, and who reflect on the creation of the heavens and the earth: "Our Lord! You have not created this in vain! Glory unto You! "Koran 3:191] "Always chanting My glories, endeavoring with great determination, bowing down before Me, these great souls perpetually worship Me with devotion [Bg.9.14]"*. The first concern is to control the senses, and since the senses cannot be controlled unless engaged in the service of the Lord, the most important duty is to engage the senses in the Lord's service. One, who is without relationship with God, can neither have a steady mind nor peace. If the senses are not engaged in the service of the Lord, they will certainly engage in material pursuits. *"Who is more astray than he who follows his lust without guidance from Allah [Koran 28:50]"?*

Chapter Six
Wherever you turn is His face

God directs everything

Nature is very mysterious and inexplicable. Often people think that either everything is created from nothing or everything has its origin in an impersonal power, called God. However, God is not just an impersonal power, for behind the power is the powerful. As a machine made of material elements cannot work without an operator, the creation is created by God and operates under His direction. Power is not the ultimate. The ultimate is the conductor of power, God, the powerful, the Supreme Person.

The Pharaoh could not acknowledge that God is the origin and director of everything. When Moses approached him, the Pharaoh was curious to know who God is. He asked Moses, *"Who is your Lord [Koran 20:49]"?* Moses' answer was that, *"My Lord is He who gave everything its existence and directs it [Koran 20:50]"*. The Pharaoh said: "*I am alone your Lord, the Most High [Koran 79:23-24]"*. The Pharaoh declared himself to be God. He refused to submit to the instructions of the Supreme Lord, as given by Moses. As a reaction to his blasphemy, severe plagues hit Egypt along with drought and famine. Finally, the Pharaoh's army was drowned in the sea [Koran 7:136]. The Pharaoh foolishly refused to accept Moses' answer and later, was completely destroyed.

In school, children are taught that everything happens automatically by nature's arrangement. That everything is executed through the machine of nature. But the laws of nature are the laws of God, for nature cannot work without the touch of God. Rain is evaporated from the oceans, takes the form of clouds, and falls to the ground. The rains then nourish the seeds which produce unlimited varieties of fruits, vegetables and grains. Does this elaborate arrangement happen by chance? The different varieties of life and of material existence do not come about by chance and necessity; they are different arrangements made by God. Varieties of life develop not by chance but by prearrangement. Because one is unable to find the real cause, one foolishly says that everything happens by chance. God is described in all scriptures of the world as the cause of all causes. His very personality is the original cause of everything, the root of everything and the seed of everything. Moses tried to explain this fact to the Pharaoh. Due to his obstinacy and rebellious spirit, he refused to accept the Lord's supreme position as the source of everyone and everything in existence, including him.

The Supreme Lord is the source and the director of everyone and everything. *"My Lord is He who gave everything its existence and directs it [Koran 20:50]"*. In the universe, everything is so perfectly ordered that only an insane man can deny that it is directed by a supreme intelligence. Things would be at random without the careful planning of God. It is a common understanding that there is a cause behind each action. A machine cannot run without an operator. In the morning and the evening, the sun is rising and setting in due course of time. It is not accidental. The sun never rises in the west and sets in the east. There must be some brain behind it, and that supreme brain is God. The words 'brain' and 'operator,' imply a person. This is explained in the Vedas: *"I am the source of all spiritual and material worlds. Everything emanates from Me. The wise who perfectly know this engage in My devotional service and worship Me with all their hearts [Bg.10.8]"*. The equilibrium of creation and its regulative actions and reactions implies the design of an intelligent brain. Seeing the wonderful activities of God suggests that a living brain gave everything its existence and directs it.

The all pervading Lord

As the birds fly in the sky as far as their capacity allows, so do the learned describe the Lord as far as their understanding allows. The Supreme Lord is unlimited. No one can know about the unlimited by his limited capacity. If great personalities cannot find adequate language to express the glories of the Lord, what can be said about the common men? It is impossible to describe the Lord fully by one's own tiny endeavor. One should submissively hear the knowledge of God as it is spoken by God Himself in the Koran and the Vedic literature. By tasting a drop of seawater one can get a general idea of the flavor of the entire ocean. Similarly, by submissively hearing about God from scriptures one can acquire some understanding of Him, although the knowledge about Him can never be complete.

The *Upaniṣhads* mark the beginning of the knowledge about God, whereas the Vedic portion dealing with fruitive activities teaches one how to fulfill his material desires by approaching different gods. The *Upaniṣhads* that are one-hundred and eight Sanskrit treatises represent the beginning of the philosophy of the Vedic teaching. The word *upa-niṣat* means "sit closely" and refers to the seeker of truth sitting closely beside his spiritual teacher in order to receive transcendental Vedic wisdom. The texts of the *Upaniṣhads* teach the philosophy about the Absolute Truth, for those who are seeking immortality. Both the soul and God are immortal. Thus, the wisdom of the *Upaniṣhads* clearly transcends the fruitive activity portions of the four Vedas. The religious aim is no longer the obtaining of earthly and heavenly happiness by worshipping the gods. The goal is the release from death by absorption in the Absolute Truth.

The followers of the Vedic sections that describe fruitive activities are totally unaware about the main problem of life which is death. Their activities are on the level of a beast, whose main hankerings are eating and sleeping. In a more advanced stage, there is awareness that this world of duality is composed of matter and spirit; that God is complete spirit without any tinge of the material qualities. In that stage there is a deep inclination to the spiritual. One cannot be saved from the cruel hands of death unless he knows what God is.

The body consists of material senses that have beginning and end. Therefore the *Upanișhads* describe the Absolute Truth as beyond the material senses that are found in this material world. If God would have material senses, He would be similar to a common man. But He does have spiritual senses. The *Śvetāśvatara Upanișad* clearly explains that the Absolute Truth has no material legs and hands but has spiritual hands. He has no material eyes, but He does have spiritual eyes that see all. He has no material ears, but He hears all, and, possesses all-perfect spiritual senses. *"Without legs and hands, He moves and accepts. Without eyes He sees, and without ears He hears. He knows all that is knowable, but no one knows Him. They call Him the original Supreme Person [*Śvetāśvatara Upanișad 3.19]*". "Everywhere is His hands and legs, His eyes, heads and faces, and He have ears everywhere. In this way the Supersoul exists, pervading everything [Bg.13:14]".*

The Koran also describes Allah as not having material senses: *"Wherever you turn, there is His face. Allah is all pervading and all knowing [Koran 2:115]"*. If Allah's senses would be material, His faces would not be all pervading. A human being with material senses cannot have his hands, his legs, his eyes, his heads and his ears everywhere. Material hands, legs, eyes, heads, faces and ears are temporary and cannot be everywhere. Consequently, Allah's hands, legs, eyes, head and ears are different from a human being, for they are all spiritual. Therefore, no interpretation should be given to the Koranic verses that describe God's hands, legs, eyes, heads, faces and ears. *"Allah sees well what you do [Koran 2:233]", "Allah hears all things [Koran 2:224]".*

Allah has no material eyes, but He does have spiritual eyes that see all that exists. Although He has no material ears, He hears everything, everywhere. Being inconceivable to material senses, the Vedas and the Koran describe the Lord without material personality. Yet Allah has a spiritual personality which is not visible or perceivable by our material senses. In our present state it is not possible to see God in His spiritual form. Our material eyes and senses cannot conceive of a spiritual form. "*But you cannot see Me with your present eyes. Therefore I give you divine eyes. Behold My mystic opulence! [Bg.11.8]*" Arjuna was given spiritual vision to see the Lord. He describes his revelation in the following two verses. O Lord, all the planets with their gods are disturbed at seeing Your great form, with its many faces, eyes, arms, thighs, legs, and bellies and Your many terrible teeth; and as they are disturbed, so am I [Bg.11:23]. O all-pervading Lord, seeing You with Your many radiant colors touching the sky, Your gaping mouths, and Your great glowing eyes, my mind is perturbed by fear. I can no longer maintain my steadiness or equilibrium of mind [Bg. 11:23]. Arjuna not only saw the Lord's faces, eyes, arms, thighs, legs, and bellies, but he also saw the whole creation with its heavens present within the Lord. Therefore, complete knowledge about God includes His manifestation of the extraordinary displays present in nature and accurate information of the Lord Himself.

I am indeed very near

Anything expressed by material vibrations, material intelligence and material senses have nothing to do with the real nature of God. The Supreme Lord is beyond the creation of this material world. He is the source of the creation. As the cause of all causes, He exists before the creation and after the creation. The Supreme Lord is the creator of everything. This means that He existed when there was no creation. *"It is I, the Supreme Lord, who was existing before the creation, when there was nothing but Myself [SB 2.9.33]"*. His name, form and qualities are not material. They are always spiritual. Therefore no one can ascertain the nature of God by material speculation, vibrations and thoughts. Only a fool can think of God as a material creation. The Supreme Personality of Godhead is not a person of the material world. No material designation can be assigned to God. For instance, poverty, old age, ugliness, ignorance is found within this material world, but in the spiritual dimension, there is no such thing as poverty, old age, ugliness, and ignorance. Being beyond His creation, the Vedas and the Koran describes Him as not having any material qualities. To show that He is beyond His creation, He is described in contradictory ways, as very near and as very far. "*I am indeed very near and listen to the prayer of every suppliant when he calls [Koran 2:186]*". "*The Supreme Lord walks and does not walk. He is far away, but He is very near as well. He is within everything, and yet He is outside of everything [Ishopanishad 5].*"

In God, there is no duality. All that exists is a product of God, and God is all perfect. A human being is subject to so many imperfections. One is limited within their body. Since it is difficult to understand the distinction between God and human beings, contradictory descriptions of the Lord are given for clarification. If someone can walk, it is illogical to say that, *'he can walk and not walk'*. But the Lord can perform both actions without having any similitude with a human being. The Supreme Lord is described as having His hands, legs, eyes, heads and ears everywhere. Due to these contradictory descriptions of God, it is very difficult to grasp the actual position of God. As the human mind has no experience of anything or anyone that is very near and very far, people either misinterpret these descriptions or reject them.

These contradictions of being very near and far are difficult to accommodate. No human being can have his hands, his legs, his eyes, his heads and his ears everywhere. In reference to the Supreme Lord, contradictory statements serve to indicate His unlimited power. Man's power is limited. Instead of thinking of the unlimited power of the Lord, one minimizes Him by denying His walking, seeing, and speaking power. Nothing is impossible for the Supreme Lord, because He is unlimited. He has unlimited power to do anything He desires. Every human being is limited by time, space and thought. However, God being unequaled is always beyond such limitations. Even the manifestation of space and time, which may appear to be the greatest, has a limitation. Through the power of thoughts, one may imagine billions and trillions of years, still it is an inadequate estimation of time. God is beyond space, time and thought. Although He seems to be within their jurisdiction, His existence transcends them.

Human's senses cannot think of the greatness of God, nor can they bring the almighty within the limitations of time and thinking power. The sun may appear invisible due to the covering of the cloud. But it is the eyes of the imperfect man below the cloud that are covered, not the sun. Muslim claim that God is great, but how would He be great if He is without legs, hands and eyes?

Arjuna saw the Lord as very near and very far in his different manifestations of extraordinary displays that are present in nature. Yet, he did not consider Him an ordinary person: "Arjuna said: You are the Supreme Personality of Godhead, the ultimate abode, the purest, the Absolute Truth. You are the eternal, transcendental, original person, the unborn, and the greatest. All the great sages such as Nārada, Asita, Devala, and Vyāsa confirm this truth about You, and now You Yourself are declaring it to me. O Krishna, I totally accept as truth all that You have told me. Neither the demigods nor the demons, O Lord, can understand Your personality"

Do not give likeness to Him

People easily relate to God as all pervading. This is true, but there is much more to God than this. To just relate to God in His all pervading feature is an indication that one's vision of God is incomplete. The aborigines of the jungle are struck with wonder by the manifestation of lightning. The potential for lightning is everywhere in the air in the form of electricity, just as the potency of fire is dormant in wood. In the manifestation of lightning, they praise God by identifying Him with an extraordinary power or attribute in nature. Aborigines are astonished by the creation of the Lord, without any factual information of the Lord Himself. God is not just a manifestation of some extraordinary display of nature. It is a fact that the manifestation of lightning is an expansion of the power of God. However, to limit one's understanding of God to a powerful lighting is not adequate. The aborigines want to see with their own eyes at once. Being unaccustomed to look unto God with a spiritual vision, they misidentify mundane lighting to be God. They do not know what the difference between matter and spirit is.

On the material level everything has its opposite. Matter is the opposite of spirit, death is the opposite of birth and beginning is the opposite of ending, and so on. In God there is no matter, beginning, end, birth and death. In Him, everything is absolutely spiritual. Therefore, the Koran states: *"Do not give likenesses to Allah [Koran 16:74]"*. Spirit and matter combine to manifest the material body. To give likeness to God means to think that God is also made with matter and spirit. In God there is not the slightest atom of matter. In God, there are no material qualities. He is full of spiritual qualities. Being beyond birth and death, beginning and end, the Supreme Lord has eternal divine qualities. This material world is the world of duality, in contrast with the oneness of God. The world of duality is composed of matter and spirit, whereas God is complete spirit without any tinge of the material qualities. The wise man, with perfect understanding of God, is he who can discriminate between matter and spirit. God is misevaluated because most people's knowledge pertains only to matter. As in modern education the knowledge about spirit is lacking, there is a great confusion.

"Do not give likenesses to Allah [Koran 16:74]" also means that God have a personal form whose qualities are not similar to a common human being. Birth, change, growth, old age and death are characteristic of material bodies. Material conditions affect those with material bodies. God's spiritual body is not subject to the six changes: birth, growth, duration, reproduction, dwindling and death. God undergoes no such changes. For God, there is no birth, no by product, no old age and no death. *"Allah, the eternal, the absolute; He begets not, nor is He begotten [Koran 112:2-3]."* The body, for example, takes birth at a certain date, and then it grows and stays for some time. From the body come so many byproducts in the form of sons and daughters, and then the body becomes old and weak, and finally when it is very old it dies. This is the law of nature. A flower is born as a bud. It grows, remains fresh for two or three days, produces a seed, gradually withers, and then it vanishes. God is not

under the jurisdiction of any element found in the law of nature. For instance, with or without air, the Lord exists eternally. Without air, no men can survive. If God is under the jurisdiction of air, then air would be greater than Him. Without air, God is still alive. He is completely transcendental to His material creation.

The parables of the slave and the dumb

God is not a mortal being, nor does He possess a body produced of matter. Some people think that if God has a body, He will be just like an ordinary living being. Not knowing His inconceivable power, such ignorant men place the Lord on an equal level with ordinary men.

To show that God is different from a mortal being, the following parable is given. *"Do not give likenesses to Allah. Allah sets forth the parable of a slave under the dominion of another with no power of any sort; and another who is bestowed with a goodly fortune and who spends from it privately and publicly. Can they be equal? God sets forth another parable of two men, a dumb person with no power of any sort and is a wearisome burden to his master. Wherever he is sent, he returns without any good. Is he equal to one who enjoins justice and is on a straight path [Koran 16:74-76]?"* God can have a human form, but one cannot compare God to a penniless and helpless slave who is under the domination of his master. Or compare God to a powerless dumb man who is burden to his master. God can have any form He desires, but His supreme power, riches, knowledge and domination over others is absolutely unlimited. A dumb person is lacking intellectual acuity, the power to speak, judge, and understand. A penniless person has not enough money to pay for his necessities. God cannot be an impoverished financially destroyed ruined flat broken penniless person. He is not a helpless slave who is under the domination of anyone. God is a person, but not a person similar to a penniless and helpless slave. He would not be a dumb wearisome person with no power of any sort and a burden to His master. God is not an ordinary person for His infinite opulence has no equal even among the powerful gods and angels. The parable of

"Do not give likenesses to Allah" shows that although God is a person, no one is equal to Him. According to this parable the definition of God is that He is the Supreme Person under no one's dominion. No one is greater than Him, or equal to Him. Although it is true that all creatures have a certain relation to God, and bear a divine impress, however, God's opulence is boundless. Therefore, God is a person, but He is not a person similar to a penniless and helpless slave. He is not a dumb wearisome person without power. He is not a burden to His master. God is not an ordinary person for His superior opulence has no equal even among the powerful gods and angels. The Lord, who is the origin of the whole creation, cannot be an ordinary human being. The Lord performs the wonderful acts of creation which is beyond any human act. *"Who sustains you (in life) from the sky and from the earth? Who has power over your hearing and your sight? Who brings out the living from the dead and the dead from the living? Who rules and regulates all affairs?" They will say, 'Allah' [Koran 10:31]".*

Chapter Seven
The Supreme Friend

The allegory of the two companions

Mysticism is a contemplative process that is meant to realize the Lord. The mystic is not just speculating about the nature of the Lord, he realizes that God is sitting within his heart[72] and the heart of all beings. Such contemplation is based on descriptions of the Lord's form as given in the revealed scriptures. Through his contemplation and prayers, the mystic tries to realize this form of the Lord within. As it is stated in the Koran and Vedic literatures: "*I have fashioned Adam and breathed into him My spirit [Koran 15:29]*". "*I am seated in everyone's heart, and from Me come remembrance, knowledge and forgetfulness [Bg.15.15]*". "*The Supreme Lord is situated in everyone's heart, O Arjuna, and is directing the wanderings of all living entities, who are seated as on a machine, made of the material energy [Bg.18.61]*".

Once Adam's body is created out of wet clay [Koran 23:12][73], the Lord entered within it. Without consciousness, the material body is like a lump of matter. As dull matter cannot work without the touch of the spirit, the Spirit of God entered within the material body of Adam. Then consciousness developed. Matter alone cannot create anything; rather, it is the power of the Spirit of God that produces things. Iron itself has no power to burn, but when iron is placed in fire, it is empowered to burn. In the ocean there are great waves moving.

Water is dull matter, but it is the air which is pushing the great waves dashing them onto the earth. Matter is activated only because of the presence of a spiritual force. Without the Spirit of God, matter cannot act. The power does not arise from matter itself but is invested by the Lord.

The all-pervading Lord is personally within everything. "*He is the Lord who eternally watches over this universe, who exists before, during and after its manifestation. He is the master of both the unmanifest material energy and the spirit soul. After sending forth the creation He enters within it, accompanying each living entity. There He creates the material bodies and then remains as their regulator [SB 10.87.50]*". The same unique Personality of Godhead exists everywhere, just like the sky. Yet, although He is within everything, He is not affected by anything. Although the sky extends everywhere and everything rests within it, the sky does not mix with anything, nor can it be divided by anything. By entering into every individual soul, God does not become divided or lose His own personality. All material objects such as air and birds, and so on are situated within the vast material sky, but the sky remains undivided. Although the sky accommodates all objects, it never mixes with anything. In the same way, God is all-pervading, but He remains individual. One may compare the Spirit of God and matter to oil mixed with water. When oil is in water, there is a distinction, and that distinction always remains.

Any material construction is nothing but a combination of matter and spirit in varied dimensions. It exists both within and beyond the body. For example, although air exists in space, it enters within each body. Similarly, God, who is the cause of creation, lives within the material world as well as beyond it. Without His presence within the material world, the creation will not develop, just as without the presence of the spirit within the physical body, the body will not grow. The creation evolves and exists because the Supreme Personality of Godhead enters it as Supersoul. God in His all-pervading feature of Supersoul enters every entity, from the biggest to the minute. Therefore the creation takes place, it grows, it gives off so many by-products, and then again it vanishes. Without His entering, nothing can exist. Without the spirit soul's entering within the body, the body cannot exist. As soon as the spirit soul goes out, the body immediately dies.

To make Adam's body active, both Adam's soul and the Spirit of God entered into it. The Koran explains that, within the same body, two companions are sitting together. Of these two companions, one is captivated to enjoy the fruits of his activities, while the other is simply witnessing the activities of His friend. The Spirit of God is the witnessing companion, and the individual soul desires to enjoy matter. Although they are companions, God is still the master and the other is the servant. *"Allah has created man. Allah knows what his soul whispers to him. Allah is nearer to him than his jugular vein. The two are meeting together. One is sitting on the right and the other on the left [Koran 50:16-17]. Whatever words he utters, a witness records it [Koran 50:18]. Each soul will come with its witness or driver [Koran 50:21]".*

These Koranic verses explain that within the body there are two kinds of souls. "*The two are meeting together' [Koran 50:17]"* is understood as referring to the Supersoul, and the individual soul. They are two companions. One is sitting on the right, God, and the other on the left, the individual soul. *Whatever words he utters, a witness records it [Koran 50:18].* A witness, the Supersoul, or God situated within the heart records whatever words the individual soul utters and whispers. The word 'record' means that the Supersoul remembers everything. There are innumerable living entities, and He is staying in them as a witness. This means that the Supersoul who is within has eyes, ears and hands everywhere, otherwise how would He hears, sees and records whatever is whispered? It should be remembered that there are innumerable individual souls. Every soul comes into the material existence with a false consciousness to lord it over matter. To fulfill their desires, the Spirit of God, does not only enter into Adam, but He enters within all forms of life. The Supersoul, God, who is seated on the right of the individual soul, is the witness who records all the mental and physical activities of the soul. The Supersoul gives the individual soul an opportunity to act freely and witnesses his activities. The Lord is present within to sanction the individual soul's desires. Without the sanction of the Supreme Soul, the individual soul cannot do anything. The individual is the sustained, and the Lord is the maintainer. The Supersoul is the knower of all past, present and future, and nothing can be concealed from Him. Under His direction only can the living being remember or forget what he might have done in the past. The witness is the Lord, and the one whose soul whispers to him is the living entity who has forgotten his real identity as a servant of God. He is overwhelmed with the dualities of happiness and distress while the Lord being neutral records all his activities. The individual soul is struggling very hard within the material body. But as soon as he agrees to voluntary accept the other companion as the supreme spiritual teacher; he immediately becomes free from all lamentations.

One may object that it is not the Supersoul, who keeps the records. It is an angel who keeps the record of the individual soul. The companion is not an angel for there is no Koranic verse that states that angels are nearer to the soul than his jugular vein. There is no Koranic verse that states that the spirit of the angel is within Adam. The Koran affirms that, it is, rather; God who is within Adam's body. "*God has breathed His spirit into Adam [Koran 15:29]".* Moreover, in Vedic literatures, there are many descriptions of the form of the Lord within the heart and many Muslim mystics have practically realized this truth. *"Being fixed, one must render service unto the Supersoul situated in one's own heart by His omnipotency. Because He is the Almighty Personality of Godhead, eternal and unlimited, He is the ultimate goal of life, and by worshiping Him one can end the cause of the conditioned state of existence [SB 2.2.6]". "Others conceive of the Personality of Godhead residing within the body in the region of the heart and measuring only eight inches, with four hands carrying a lotus, a wheel of a chariot, a conchshell and a club respectively. His mouth expresses His happiness. His eyes spread like the petals of a lotus, and His garments, yellowish like the saffron of a kadamba flower, are bedecked with valuable jewels. His ornaments are all made of gold, set with jewels, and He wears a glowing head dress and earrings. He is well decorated with an ornamental wreath about His waist and rings studded with valuable jewels on His fingers.*

His leglets, His bangles, His oiled hair, curling with a bluish tint, and His beautiful smiling face are all very pleasing. The Lord's magnanimous pastimes and the glowing glancing of His smiling face are all indications of His extensive benedictions. One must therefore concentrate on this transcendental form of the Lord, as long as the mind can be fixed on Him by meditation. The process of meditation should begin from the lotus feet of the Lord and progress to His smiling face. The meditation should be concentrated upon the lotus feet, then the calves, then the thighs, and in this way higher and higher. The more the mind becomes fixed upon the different parts of the limbs; one after another, the more the intelligence becomes purified [SB 2.2.8-13]".

The Supersoul that resides within the body and the individual soul are not formless. They both have a spiritual form. The Supersoul has His hands, legs, eyes, ears, and faces everywhere, whereas the individual soul, which is within the material body, has two hands, two legs, two eyes, two ears, and one face. Just as a shirt and coat cover the body the spirit soul is covered by the material body. It is because the spiritual body has a shape that the material body also takes a shape. The material body is like a dress. The soul is covered by an external dress which is not his real body. The garments of the body are the misconception that one is a product of matter. At present, the spirit soul is within this material body, but originally the spirit soul had no material body. When the material body is annihilated, the spiritual body of the spirit soul eternally exists. In spiritual consciousness, one is free from all such material designations. That freedom is achieved when one's consciousness is constantly in touch with God through His words. Moreover, the individual soul is present only within his particular body, whereas the Supersoul is present in each and every body. "*Wherever you turn, there is His face [Koran 2:115]"* The Supersoul has His hands, legs, eyes, ears, and heads and faces everywhere. Allah through His expansion as Supersoul is situated within all living beings including the gods, human beings and animals. The individual soul cannot have his hands, his legs, his eyes, and his ears everywhere. The individual soul knows only about his own thinking, feeling and willing activities. The Supersoul, the witness, being present everywhere, knows everyone's thinking, feeling and willing activities.

While the Koran gives the allegory of two companions, Vedic literatures declare that there are two birds in one tree. One of them is eating the fruits of the tree, while the other witnesses his actions. The witness is the Lord, and the fruit-eater is the living entity [Śvetāśvatara Upaniṣad 4.6]. "*Both the Supersoul and the individual soul are situated on the same tree of the body within the same heart of the living being. Only one who has become free from all material desires as well as lamentations can, by the grace of the Supreme, understand the glories of the soul [Kaṭha Upaniṣhad (1,2.20)]". Although the two birds are in the same tree, the eating bird is fully engrossed with anxiety and moroseness as the enjoyer of the fruits of the tree. But if in some way or other he turns his face to his friend who is the Lord and knows His glories—at once the suffering bird becomes free from all anxieties [Muṇḍaka Upaniṣad 3.1.2]; [Śvetāśvatara Upaniṣad 4.7]".* The allegory of two birds in the same tree illustrates that within the heart God and the soul reside. Just as a bird makes a nest in a tree, the soul sits within the heart. The example is suitable because the bird is always distinct from the tree. Similarly, God and the soul are distinct entities, separate from the temporary material body. The Lord is not interested in the bitter fruits of material activities, whereas the ordinary conditioned soul busily consumes such bitter fruits, thinking them to be sweet. Ultimately, the fruit of all material endeavors is death, but the soul foolishly thinks that it will bring him everlasting happiness.

The Koran uses the word 'two companions' whereas the Vedic texts use the word 'two friends'. The real friend or companion is the Lord, who is situated within the heart. It is only He who can give real happiness. The Lord is so kind that He patiently sits in the heart, trying to guide the conditioned soul to come back to Him. Certainly no material friend would remain with his foolish companion for a life time. Especially if his companion were to ignore him or even curse him. But the Lord is such a kind, faithful, loving friend that He is present even in the heart of the insect, hog and dog. Although sitting as friends, God keep His superior position. *"By chance, two birds have made a nest together in the same tree. The two birds are friends and are of a similar nature. One of them, however, is eating the fruits of the tree, whereas the other, who does not eat the fruits, is in a superior position due to His potency [SB 11.11.6]".* At birth, the individual soul, due to his forgetfulness of God, identifies himself with a particular body. After assuming a material form, he is enwrapped in ignorance. His natural opulences become almost extinct. However, although the Supersoul appears within this material world, His opulences are not diminished. He maintains all opulences and perfections in full while He keeps Himself apart from all the tribulations of this material world. The conditioned soul engages in the happiness and distress of the body. He becomes subjected to varieties of misfortunes. Being deprived of the eternal service to the Lord, he becomes illusioned in many ways. Because he has neglected the service of the Lord, he is therefore put in the service of matter. He is still serving, but in a perverted manner.

The Supersoul is beyond sinful or pious activities. God is above the law, He makes the law. These laws are meant for the rectification of the rebellious souls in the material world, so that they can again develop the desire to serve the Lord and return to Him. The sun, which is situated in a specific location, is reflected in countless jewels and appears in innumerable localized aspects. Similarly, God, although eternally present in His Kingdom, is reflected in everyone's heart as the Supersoul. The Vedic literatures and the Koran explain that, the Supersoul, who is sitting along with the soul in the body, always tries to give guidance to the individual soul. The Supersoul is waiting for the time when the soul is ready to give up all material desires and submit to His will. Through his contemplation and prayers, the mystic tries to see that God along with the subordinate soul is present in every living being.

Individuality

Every soul is the owner of a specific body. Everyone is conscious of the happiness and distress of his own body, but not of other bodies. Consciousness, which permeates the whole body, is limited within one's personal body. Each and every body is the embodiment of an individual soul. The symptom of the soul's presence is perceived as individual consciousness. As the sun is situated in one place but is illuminating the whole universe, so the spirit soul illuminates the whole body by consciousness. Thus consciousness is a testimony of the presence of the soul, as sunshine or light is the proof of the presence of the sun. *"As the sun alone illuminates all this universe, so does the living entity, one within the body, illuminate the entire body by consciousness [Bg.13.34]". "As the fragrance of flowers or other objects travel to a place far from its source, so the consciousness that emanates from the soul travels from the heart and enter the head, feet, or other parts of the body [Kauśitaki Upaniṣhad 3.6]". "By consciousness the soul is all-pervading in the material body74."*

The position of God is that of supreme consciousness. The living entities are also conscious. But they cannot be supremely conscious at any stage of life. They are by nature very limited, while God is unlimited. The living being is conscious of his particular body, whereas the Lord is conscious of all bodies. He lives in the heart of every living being, He is conscious of all the mental movements of a particular soul. What is spread all over the body is consciousness. If a lamp is brought in a dark room, darkness will be immediately vanquished. Similarly, the soul is like a lamp from which emanate the light of consciousness. Once the soul enters a material body consciousness spread all over it. Within a dead body there is no light because the soul, along with consciousness that was illuminating the body has left. Abraham wanted to understand the subject of the soul, therefore he asked the Lord to give him the knowledge about death and life. *"Abraham asked Allah, 'show me how You give death and life'. Allah asked him to take four birds and cut their bodies to pieces. Scatter them over the mountain-tops, and then call them back. They will come swiftly to you [Koran 2:260]".* When Abraham called the four birds that he has cut to so many pieces, only four birds with four souls came. If their soul would have been cut to pieces, many birds would have come. But only four birds have come back. Death affects the body, not the soul. The Lord could have asked Abraham to just kill the four birds. But He asked him to cut the bodies of the four birds to so many pieces to show that the soul cannot be cut to pieces. Each bird is an individual spirit soul. The body may be cut to so many pieces, but no one will be able to cut the soul. The Vedic literatures state similar teaching. *"The soul can never be cut to pieces by any weapon, nor burned by fire, nor moistened by water, nor withered by the wind [Bg.2:23]"*. The soul cannot be killed by any kinds of weapons such as swords, flame, water, fire, nuclear weapons and tornado. The soul can never be cut into pieces, nor annihilated by any kind of weapons. The individual souls are eternally separated parts of God. *"When the trumpet is blown; this is the day of the threatening [Koran 50:20]. Every soul will come, along with it a driver and a witness [Koran 50:21]. Certainly you were heedless of it (the Koran), but now We have removed from you your veil, so your sight today is sharp [Koran 50:22].* The soul is eternally individual. When covered by matter, the soul leaves the Kingdom of the Supreme Lord. Just as the sparks of a fire, although one in quality with the fire, are prone to be extinguished when out of the fire. Even in heaven, the soul has a separate identity, as is evident from the teachings of the Lord to Abraham. The soul remains the same eternally, without change. The air can gradually evaporate a big ocean, but the soul is never annihilated. It is indestructible, and immutable. *"This individual soul is unbreakable and insoluble, and can be neither burned nor dried. He is everlasting, present everywhere, unchangeable, immovable and eternally the same [Bg. 2.25]."*

There are so many thinkers who claim that God was one, but under the effect of ignorance and evil, He divided into so many souls. They claim that at present everyone is God. Once this ignorance is removed, all the souls that were divided will again join together and make one God. The Pharaoh was an adept of this belief. He was curious to know who God is. As he was lacking knowledge, he taught that He was God. The Pharaoh said: "*I am alone your Lord, the Most High [Koran 79:23-24]"*. Moses tried to explain to him that God is an individual person who directs everything, but the dull minded Pharaoh could not understand. Moses' answer was that, *"My Lord is He who gave everything its existence and directs it [Koran 20:50]"*. The creator must be an individual living being just as the maker of clay pots is a conscious individual potter. In each and every affair of the cosmology, the foolish takes everything to be dead stone without being manipulated by a supreme intelligent person. Matter is dead but God is not a dead stone, nor is He inactive. In the Koran there are many verses that show that everything is done under His direction. As it is said, not a blade of grass moves without His sanction. *"Allah, there is no god but He, the living, the self-subsisting, the eternal. Neither slumber no sleep can seize Him. Whatever is in the heavens and whatever is in the earth is His. Who is he that can intercede with Him except by His permission? He knows past and present while they encompass nothing of His knowledge save what He will. His throne includes the heavens and the earth. He is never weary to preserve them. He is the sublime, the tremendous [Koran 2:255]"*. God is always conscious. He is never out of consciousness, either in dream or sleep.

Individuality does not arise only when the soul comes in contact with the body or the mind. The soul is by nature individual. After the destruction of the material body, individuality is kept. Every soul is endowed with a special feeling, Knowledge, sight and movement. These are inherent qualities in the soul. The soul is not like an iron that assumes the quality of fire when placed in fire. Either in the awakening, sleeping or death state the soul is always endowed with spiritual qualities. *"Neither slumber no sleep can seize Him [Koran 2:255]". "The soul's consciousness is never destroyed [Bṛhad-āraṇyaka Upaniṣad 4.5.14]"*. The soul obscures its natural spiritual knowledge by deliberately avoiding God and revives its natural spiritual consciousness by turning to God. This is described in Vedic wisdom. *"As by washing away the dirt that covered a jewel, the jewel's splendor is not created but merely uncovered, so by removing the dirt of materialism that covered the soul, the soul's splendor is not created, but merely uncovered. As by digging a well, water is brought forth but not created, so by spiritual activities the nature of the soul is brought forth but not created. How would it be possible to create the soul's qualities from nothing? When material faults are destroyed, the soul's qualities become revealed. The soul's qualities are eternal. They are never created75."* As Vedic knowledge gives the analogy of the dirt that covers a jewel and the digging of water, similarly the Koran sates that the eyes, the heart and the ears are covered. Once these covering are removed individual consciousness manifest but not created *"Allah has set a seal on their hearts and on their hearing, and on their eyes is a veil [Koran 2:7]. He makes you, in the wombs of your mothers, in stages, one after another, in three veils of darkness [Koran 39:6]"*.

God is knowledge and consciousness personified. The soul is consciousness and conscious of itself. By the presence of consciousness, the presence of the soul is verified. Once consciousness leaves the body, the material body becomes active. Consciousness is perceived, by activities. Consciousness cannot be silent, even for a moment. When the body does not act, the consciousness acts in the form of dreams. One can remain unconsciousness for a limited period with the help of drug. When their effect is finished one is awake, the consciousness again acts earnestly. The soul's individuality exists as the soul exists. Individuality is never destroyed. As the soul exists eternally, without beginning and end, the soul's individuality eternally exists. The sun may be given here as an example. As long as the sun exists it will have light and heat, which are actually non different from the sun. Similarly as long as the soul exists both consciousness and individuality exist. It is not that individuality is non-existent in death and only exists in birth. Individuality is fully manifested both at birth and death. In the state of death, individuality exists as an intrinsic nature of the soul. At death, there are many descriptions in the Koran and Vedic literatures about the punishment or the enjoyment of the soul in the hellish or heavenly planets. The state of death is similar to a state of deep sleep. One may also think that in deep sleep individual consciousness is nonexistent. When there is no object for consciousness to perceive, in deep sleep individuality is dormant. When the senses are awake individual consciousness becomes manifested. Had it not existed in a dormant state during deep sleep, individual consciousness would not have manifested itself in the waking state? A eunuch cannot manifest virility at in adulthood. In childhood virility and other qualities associated with it exist in a dormant state. At the beginning of adulthood, they become manifested. In the same way individuality is dormant in deep sleep and fully manifested in the waking state. Individuality is not created by contact with the senses because if the soul is all-pervading then it would be always in contact with the senses. Moreover, if the individual spirit soul were all-pervading then everyone would simultaneously feel the pains and pleasures of everyone else. If this were so there would be no meaning to individual experience, individual desire and individual destiny. The individual spirit soul is not all pervading. It is atomic in size and different from each other material bodies. Although atomic in size, the individual spirit soul can act in any place, but not simultaneously in every place. By its individual quality, the spirit soul can pervade its material body. It can perceive the happiness and the distress and other sensations present in the various parts of its material body. Not in other bodies.

Individuality does not end with either the death of the mortal body or salvation. The soul is eternally an individual, past, present and future. The Koran explains that one, who had existed in the past, will continue to exist in the future. *"How do you deny God and you were dead and He gave you life? Again He will cause you to die and again bring you to life, and then you shall be brought back to Him [Koran 2:28]"*. After the death of this material body, one will continue to exist. The body is finished, but the soul is not finished. When the body vanishes, it decomposes and returns to nature. A pot is produced from the earth, and when broken or destroyed the pot again mingles with its original ingredients, the earth. The soul, according to auspicious and inauspicious deeds, goes either to the heaven, hell or the Kingdom of God.

The soul is different from the material ingredient. In the material world even iron and gold can be melted and cut to pieces, but these laws do not apply to the spirit soul. The soul can neither be melted nor cut into pieces. Matter interacts with matter, but the soul is above material action and reaction. Because it is not possible to cut the soul, it is not possible to sever the individuality of the soul. The soul cannot be cut from God and again join together. Even if it is joined, the soul keeps a separate identity. Just like a green bird, when he enters into the tree, it retains its identity as a bird, although it appears to merge with the greenness of the tree. The present material body is covered by many garments in the form of shirt and the coat, yet it is not mixed up. As the material body keeps always separate identity from cloths, likewise the soul always keeps separate identity from the material covering. As confirmed by the Lord in the Vedas, all individual souls are eternally separated parts of Him; all the souls are His "eternal fragments." *"The living entities in this conditional world are My fragmental parts, and they are eternal. But due to conditioned life, they are struggling very hard with the six senses, which include the mind [Bg. 15.7]."* Both God and all souls are individuals. *"He is the Supreme, above His servants [Koran 6.18]".* One aspect of spiritual individuality is that a soul relates to the Lord as a servant. Each soul is a separate and distinct being with an individual relationship with God. The soul is not simply light or existence. It is an individual which has an individual relationship with God. Vedic literatures directly refer to the unending nature of individuality and the immortality of the soul. Lord Krishna told Arjuna, *"Never was there a time when I did not exist, nor you, nor all these kings; nor in the future shall any of us cease to be [Bg.2.12]."*

Even animals and trees are individual souls. Birds fly in the sky because within their body there is the spirit soul. "*Jesus created from clay the form of a bird and by His permission, he breathed into it, and it became a flying bird [Koran 5:110]".* Because of the presence of a pilot a big airplane flies without any difficulty in the sky. The flying power does not merely depend on the mechanical arrangement of the engineer, but a living person must pilot the plane. A tree gradually grows and gives flowers and fruits because of the presence of the spirit soul. A tree grows as long as there is life in it. Some Koranic verses narrate that trees glorify God. *"The grass and trees bow to Him in adoration [Koran 55:6]".* As stated in the Vedic literature, all the trees, overloaded with fruits and fresh twigs, bent down to glorify the Lord[76]. Without the spirit soul, trees cannot grow. When any material object displays growth, it must be understood that there is a spirit soul within it.

People often think that animals and trees have no soul because they do not have a very developed consciousness. It is a fact that there is a great difference between the consciousness of human beings, trees and animals. Human beings have a higher intelligence and more developed consciousness. Animals and trees have less intelligence and emotions. If a tree is cut to pieces, it will show no resistance. An animal will loudly scream when his body is cut. As an individual exhibits a personal physical appearance, similarly the identity of a soul also exists on a spiritual level. Each soul is a separate and distinct being with a unique and individual relationship with God. The realized mystic experiences this relationship. Every soul has an eternal, individual relationship with the Supreme Person that becomes clearer and clearer as by serving the Lord. The common ground shared by the whole group is the satisfaction of the Lord, not the mere satisfaction of oneself. If one is guided by the principles of the revealed scriptures, one will develop a personal individual relationship with the Supreme. While working for the Lord, one feels the touch of the Supreme.

A friend to all

The mystic does not make any distinction between community, nation, caste or species, for God, as Supersoul, is present within everyone. Everyone should be given proper respect, and no living being should be neglected. As one offers respect to God, one should similarly offer proper respect to each and every living being because God dwells within everybody. As Supersoul, the Lord is equally kind to everyone. He maintains every living being with great consideration. Due to this deep realization, the mystic has equal vision towards all beings. *"The humble sages, by virtue of true knowledge, see with equal vision a learned and gentle brāhmaṇa, a cow, an elephant, a dog and a dog-eater. [Bg 5.18]"*

One may question that if God is inside every moving being including animals, why does He allow animal slaughtering? The Vedic literatures allow animal slaughtering for those who are too much attached to meat eating. Among the thirty three million gods that the Vedas describe, flesh can be offered only to goddess Kālī Mā. She, however, does not partake of these remnants, but distributes them to her associates who have demoniac forms. Other gods totally refuse any meat offering. The Koran shares similar idea. "*It is not the flesh and blood that reaches Allah, it is your sanctities that reaches Him [Koran 22:37]*". The Vedic literatures, however, do not sanction the mass slaughter of animals as is seen in modern slaughterhouses. They are many rules and regulations stipulated in the process of sacrificing animals. Once a month on the night of the full moon, a goat may be sacrificed. The slaughtered animal cannot be sold to others. One is not allowed to buy meat from a butcher. At present, most animals are killed in slaughterhouses. Such killing is most sinful because it is done as a business, without taking into consideration religious rites given in scripture.

The mystic, knowing that God resides within all bodies wherein there is life, never indulges in meat eating. He is a friend to all. The following Koranic verse states that within the living body of animals is the soul: "*Jesus created from clay the form of a bird and by His permission, he breathed into it, and it became a flying bird [Koran 5:110]*". Islam also recommends sacrifice under certain rules and regulations. The person who holds the animal and the person, who slaughters it, have to observe the ritual of praying five times a day. They have to perform their ablutions, feed water to the animal and turn the head of the animal in the direction of Mecca. The person who slaughters the animal must look into the eyes of the animal; recite a prayer in Arabic known as Kālīmā before cutting its neck. While cutting, he has to continually look into the eyes of the animal until its soul departs, and repeat the Kālīmā all the while. After cutting the neck, he has to keep looking into the animal's eyes and watch his tears until it dies. The purpose behind all these rules is to change the heart of the man who is slaughtering the animal, hoping that one day; he will develop compassion for the animal and stop this killing business[77].

From the above description one has to realize that animal sacrifice is a risky business. Although the Vedic literatures allow meat eating under certain rules and regulations, they do not recommend it. For one who is a serious believer, meat eating hinders one's spiritual advancement. Meat eating is contradictory to the idea of realizing God within all living beings.

For the true benefit of everyone, vegetables, grains, fruits and milk are the proper foods for human beings. Eating is an essential activity for the human being for the maintenance of the body. To be healthy, it is not necessary, or even beneficial, to eat non-vegetarian food. As early as 1961, the Journal of the American Medical Association stated that ninety to ninety-seven percent of heart disease, the cause of more than one half of the deaths in the United States, could be prevented by a vegetarian diet[78]. In his Notes on the Causation of Cancer, Rollo Russell writes, "I have found of twenty-five nations eating flesh largely, nineteen had a high cancer rate and only one had a low rate, and that of thirty-five nations eating little or no flesh, not one had a high rate[79]."

Many animals are herbivores, they don't eat meat. Human beings have the superior intelligence to understand that all the varieties of foodstuffs that are available to him are the most merciful arrangement of God. One who takes his food, without first acknowledging that it is God who supplies all our necessities of life, eats only sin. As blood and flesh does not reach Allah [Koran 22:37], all scriptures of the world recommend that vegetarian foodstuffs should be offered to God. *"If one offers Me with love and devotion a leaf, a flower, fruit or water, I will accept it [Bg. 9:26]".* Offering vegetarian foodstuff to God is a process that nourishes the soul, promoting compassion and dedication to God in the heart of the living being. An example supporting vegetarianism is also presented in the Koran. For instance, the Lord gave the Children of Israel sanctified vegetarian foodstuff, but they asked for non sanctified food mixed with onion and garlic. And they were covered with humiliation and subject to miseries. *"One day they said, 'O Moses, we cannot endure one kind of food; ask your Lord to give us what the earth grows, of its herbs, cucumbers, garlic, lentils and onions." Moses said: 'would you like to exchange what is good with what is bad? Go then to the city and you shall have what you ask'. They were covered with humiliation and misery, earning the wrath of God, for they disbelieved the word of God [Koran 2:61]".*

Eating sanctified vegetarian food that is prepared for the pleasure of the Lord is a very simple method for reviving one's relationship with God. That is the sum and substance of the Vedas. The ultimate purpose of the Vedas is to know Him only. One may argue that the Vedic activities are based on sacrificial ceremonies. That is true. But all such sacrifices are meant for realizing the truth about the Supreme Lord. The Lord says, *"All that you do, all that you eat, all that you offer and give away, as well as all austerities that you may perform, should be done as an offering unto Me [Bg.9.27]."* One who first offers his prepared vegetables, fruits, grains and milk to God is released from all sins. *"The devotees of the Lord are released from all kinds of sins because they eat food which is offered first for sacrifice. Others, who prepare food for personal sense enjoyment, verily eat only sin [Bg.3.13]".* Beyond the concerns of health, the offering of sanctified vegetarian foodstuffs to God has a higher spiritual dimension that can help one develop his natural relationship for God. One who reawakens his eternal relationship with God becomes a true mystic, a friend to all living beings.

The path of renunciation

In the Koran and the Vedas two paths for spiritual advancement are described. One permits regulated sense enjoyment according to the scriptures. The other recommends the path of renouncing the fruits of one's work for the satisfaction of God. *"Some of you desired this world and some of you desired the next [Koran 3:152]". "In the Vedas there are directions for two kinds of activities, activities for those who are attached to material enjoyment and activities for those who are materially detached [SB 4.4.20]".* Although the Vedic texts allow regulated and limited sense enjoyment for gradual spiritual advancement, the path of enjoyment is inferior for material enjoyment is temporary and illusory. Material enjoyment results in misery and frustration. The path of sacrifice for the supreme cause is superior for it leads to eternal life of devotional service in the Kingdom of God.

The path of renouncing sense enjoyment is described in the Koran. "*Eat and enjoy for a little while [Koran 77:46]. When will you realize that, 'Of no profit to me has been my wealth' [Koran 69:28]? O believers, your wives and your children are certainly enemies to yourselves. So beware of them [Koran 64:14]. Your wealth and your children are only trial. With Allah is the highest reward [Koran 64:15]. O you, who believe, let not your wealth and your children divert you from the remembrance of Allah [Koran 63:9]*". These verses illustrate the temporary nature of material attachments and enjoyment. Excessive attachment to family members increases one's attraction to the material world. To diminish such attraction, the above Koranic verses imply that God should be the center of activities.

The individual often wants to win over material existence, with the help of bodily strength, children, wife, relatives, etc. One does not see that his family members are all destined to death. One should examine the fact that his father or his father's father has already died. Next, one should understand that he and his children are destined to die. No one will survive in this struggle for life. Our relatives are not only mortal, but often bewildered by ignorance. The duty of the believer is to reach the path of renunciation. Those who are engaged in the path of sense enjoyment are bewildered by some Koranic verses that encourage sense enjoyment. The real believer, who is anxious to come back to the Kingdom of God, is not bewildered for he knows the real meaning of the Koranic verses: "*Fair in the eyes of men is the love of things they covet. Women and sons, and hoarded heaps of gold and silver; well bred horses, tilled land and cattle. These are the possessions of this world. The best of the goals is to return to God [Koran 3:14]. A brief enjoyment, and then their abode is hell; an evil resting-place [Koran 3:17]*".

The history of human society definitely proves it. Prosperous empires and great civilization such as the Roman Empire, the Mogul Empire and the British Empire have vanished with the passing of time. The foolish want to live perpetually with the help of material technology without putting God in the center. Any aristocracy, any social prestige or any advancement of material civilization without God is like the decoration of a dead body. Sometimes when a relative dies, the dead body is made more attractive by putting on nice clothes, ornaments and even makeup and then taken on procession. But that sort of decoration has no actual value for the soul is already gone. Modern society is vastly ignorant to the nature of the soul. This lack of the knowledge of the soul exhibited by human society is certainly misleading. It is all due to ignoring the fact that one is a living soul. The living soul is always different from the material body. Victimized by ignorance, one in vain searches after permanent living conditions, which is impossible to find in this material world.

If one desires freedom from the inauspicious path of sense enjoyment, one must cease to act as a sense enjoyer. One who wants to reach the path of renunciation has to first stop killing animals. An animal-killer cannot relish the glories of God. Therefore if one wants to be educated in the path of renunciation, he has first to understand that spiritual realization and animal-killing go ill together. In one conversation between Shri Chaitanya Mahāprabhu and Maulānā Sirājuddina Chand Kazi the issue of renunciation and animal slaughter was discussed. Shri Chaitanya Mahāprabhu said, "My dear uncle, I have come to your home just to ask you some questions". "Yes," Maulānā Sirājuddina replied, "You are welcome. Just tell me what is in your mind." [CC Ādi 17.152]. Shri Chaitanya Mahāprabhu said, "You drink cows' milk; therefore the cow is like your mother. And the bull produces grains for your maintenance; therefore he is like your father [CC Ādi 17.153]. "Since the bull and cow are like your father and mother, how can you kill and eat them? What kind of religious principle is this? On what strength are you so daring that you commit such sinful activities [CC Ādi 17.154]?" Maulānā Sirājuddina replied, "As you have your scriptures called the Vedas, we have our scripture, known as the holy Koran [CC Ādi 17.155]. "According to the Koran, there are two ways of advancement: the path of increasing the propensity to enjoy called the path of sense enjoyment, and the path of decreasing the propensity to enjoy called the path of renunciation. On the path of renunciation, killing of animals is prohibited [CC

Ādi 17.156]. In the above dialogue, Maulānā Sirājuddina, clearly confirms that on the path of renunciation, meat eating is rejected.

The path of sense enjoyment is called the materialistic way of life. In material existence, one always works very hard but is ultimately baffled. On the path of sense enjoyment, every living being is subject to five different states of suffering: hard labor, stress, frustration, fear, and death. When one is involved in very hard labor, the body and mind are put under stress. For example, sometimes we see a horse foaming at the mouth with heavy labor. Similarly, when one is tired from working very hard, their tongue may become dry and some foam may forms in their mouth. Despite working so hard, one is always fearful about the outcome of the work. At the end, one is disappointed. Finally, all hopes and plans to secure material happiness end with death. When there is an attempt to nullify these five different states of suffering, one reaches the level of the path of renunciation[80]. One realizes that the path of sense enjoyment is full of tribulation. The path of renunciation is superior for it leads to the Kingdom of God, where there is no labor, no stress, no frustration, no fear, and no death.

Chapter Eight
The Kingdom of God

The parables of the lantern and the fire

To establish a relationship with God is necessary, for every living being is related to the Lord. In this regard, the hankering of Moses to see the face of God is evidence that the desire to know God lies dormant in all living beings. Though Moses was not granted God's vision, he saw the effulgence of the Lord. *"Moses said, 'O my Lord, show yourself to me that I may look upon you'. 'You cannot behold Me,' Allah said. 'But look at the mountain; if it remains firm in its place, you may then behold Me.' When Allah appeared on the mountain as His effulgence, it crumbled to a heap of dust. And Moses fell unconscious. When he came to his senses, he said, All glories to you, I turn to you in repentance, and I am the first to believe' [Koran 7:143]."* At first Allah told Moses, 'you cannot behold Me', then He again told him, *'you can see Me, if the mountain remains firm in its place'*. Moses could see God in His formless aspect as His effulgence in the form of light. Having a form and being formless, Allah can be seen and not seen, according to one's level of perception.

The Supreme Lord is the source of light. In the Vedic literatures and the Koran it is stated that in the Kingdom of God there is no need of sun or moon, because the effulgence of the Supreme Lord is there. *"Allah is the Light of the heavens and the earth [Koran 24:35]"*. "*It is He who gives the sun its radiance, the moon its luster [Koran 10:5]" "He is the source of light in all luminous objects [Bg.13:18]". "I am the light of the sun and the moon [Bg.7:8]".* In the material world the assistance of sun, moon, electricity, etc., for light is required. But in the kingdom of God there is no need of such things. In the material world, the light of the sun and the moon is not independent. The real source of light is the effulgence, which diffuses light from the transcendental body of the Lord. That same light is reflected as the light of the sun and the light of the moon. His brilliantly glowing body is the source of immeasurable spiritual light[81].

As the all pervading sunshine emanates from the sun globe, God's effulgence emanates from God's spiritual body. When one describes the sun, one includes the sunshine for the sunshine emanates from the sun. Likewise, behind Allah's effulgence, is God's spiritual body that is the source of light. The following Koranic parable explains more clearly this truth. "*Allah is the light of the heavens and the earth. The parable of His light is as a lantern* in *which there is a light. The light enclosed in glass is as brilliant as a star. Kindled from a blessed tree, an olive, neither of the east nor of the west, whose oil* would *almost glow forth (of itself), though no fire touched it. Light upon light [Koran 24:35]".*

This parable describes Allah as the light of the heavens and the earth. The parable of His light is similar to a lantern from which light is emanating through a glass that is as brilliant as a star. In this parable the analogy of the lantern represents God. And the light which emanates from the lantern represents God's effulgence. The Vedas also give a parable that very much parallels the above Koranic parable: *"As a fire, although existing in one place, can expand its light and heat everywhere, so the omnipotent Lord, although situated in His spiritual abode, expands Himself everywhere, in both the material and spiritual worlds, by His various energies [Viṣṇu Purāṇa 1.22.52]".*

To understand the nature of God, the above Koranic parable gives the example of a lantern whereas Vedic literatures give the example of fire. Both a lantern and fire are localized whereas the light that emanates from them is all pervading. The Supreme Lord is present as the localized Supersoul in the heart of every living being and He also exists in His Kingdom. The all-pervading aspect is God's effulgence. A fire and lantern consist of three elements: heat and light, which are the energy of the fire, and the fire itself. The symptoms of fire are exhibited through the light and heat. Fire is situated in one place, whiles the heat and light produced by the fire pervade to a far distance place. As the heat and light of the fire are separate, likewise God's spiritual body and His effulgence are separate. Although one cannot differentiate fire from heat and light, but still distinction is there. Fire is a reality and the heat and light are simply the fire's energy. As heat and light are formless energies of the fire, but only fire has form. Similarly, Allah's effulgence is formless and God's spiritual body from where the effulgence emanates has a real form. As fire is the real form of the heat and light, Allah's form is a reality. As heat and light cannot be taken from fire, Allah's form cannot be separated from His effulgence. As without heat and light, there is no meaning to the word fire, without Allah having form there is no question of Allah's effulgence. When fire is kindled one can see that it has form, it makes sound and brings warmth to the skin. Allah, who causes fire, has also a form, sound and a touch. If a form, speech and touch were missing in Allah, these qualities would not be present in the fire, because fire has its ultimate origin in Allah. God is described as the light of the heavens and earth [Koran 24:35]. Since the sunshine is the luster of the sun planet, by seeing the sun one automatically sees the sunshine. Similarly, by seeing the Supreme Personality of Godhead one simultaneously experiences the effulgence of His bodily luster. The Lord's all-pervasiveness is due to His illumination everywhere. We have experience that the sun is situated in one place, but the sunlight is diffused all around for millions and millions of miles. Similarly, although the supreme light is situated in His personal abode, the Kingdom of God, His light is diffused everywhere.

Allah is called the 'light of light' because His light is like a pure fire without flame, without smoke and without sparks. No one has ever experienced in this material world a fire without flame, smoke and sparks. For instance, the light of an electrical bulb has flame, smoke and sparks emanating from the filament of the light bulb. The Koran explains that Allah's light is not an ordinary light. The oil that illuminates the lantern is self-illuminating. It does not require fire to kindle it nor does it require a continuous supply of oil, the supply is inexhaustible. In the material world there is no oil that glows forth of itself without kindling and replenishes itself without limit.: "*Kindled from a blessed tree, an olive, neither of the east nor of the west, whose oil* would *almost glow forth (of itself), though no fire touched it. Light upon light [Koran 24:35]"*.

While God's effulgence expands as light, God does not lose His individuality. He remains distinct from His creation. This is stated in the Vedic literatures as follow: *"God is perfect and complete, and because He is completely perfect, all emanations from Him, such as this material creation, are perfectly equipped as complete wholes [Ishopanishad Invocation]."* Although everything emanates from God, His powers never diminish. As the supply of oil from the blessed olive tree that lights the lantern is inexhaustible, His influence expands throughout the universe without losing His individuality. His unlimited powers are complete in themselves.

The abode of God contains many mansions

It has been stated before that the Supreme Lord is the source of light. That in the kingdom of God there is no need of sun or moon. The real source of light is God's effulgence, which diffuses light from the transcendental body of the Lord. This is confirmed in the following verse: *"That supreme abode of Mine is not illumined by the sun or moon, nor by fire or electricity [Bg.15.6]"*.

"Yet there is another unmanifest nature, which is eternal and is transcendental to this manifested and unmanifested matter. It is supreme and is never annihilated. When all in this world is annihilated, that part remains as it is [Bg. 8.20]". "His Throne does extend over the heavens and the earth [Koran 2:255]".

The Supreme Lord is beyond the material creation. The universe is one of the material creations, but God is transcendental to such material creation. Everything that is created, sustained, and at the end annihilated is known as the material world. The existence of God, His name, form, attributes, etc. are not within the jurisdiction of the material world. The Koran explains that, according to one's deeds, the soul, which is within the material creation, will reach three kinds of destinations: The companions of the right hand that achieve the heavenly planets [Koran 56:8], the companions of the left hand that enter into the hellish planets [Koran 56:9] and the foremost [Koran 56:10] who will be the nearest to God [Koran 56:12] and enter into His Kingdom.

The Koran gives a full description of the Kingdom of God. The foremost will be honored [Koran 56:11] in gardens of bliss [Koran 56:12]. A multitude of those of old time will be foremost, ranking above all others [Koran 56:13] and very few among the later time [Koran 56:14].

"You shall be sorted out into three classes: The companions of the right hand. How happy will be the companions of the right hand. The companions of the left hand, how wretched will be the companions of the left hand. The foremost who will be the nearest to God will be in garden of bliss; a multitude of people among old time and a few among the later time [Koran 56.7-14]. They will be on thrones encrusted (with gold and precious stones) [Koran 56.15]. They will be served by immortal boys [Koran 56.17]. With bowls and ewers and a cup from a pure spring [Koran 56.18]. They shall not be affected with headache thereby, nor shall they get exhausted [Koran 56.19]. There will be companions with beautiful, big, and lustrous eyes like unto hidden pearls [Koran 56.20]. Reward for what they used to do [Koran 56.24]. They will hear no frivolity there or vain and sinful discourse [Koran 56.25].

The Vedic texts give an elaborate description of God's abode. The kingdom of God is the residence of God and His servants[82]. There is no question of birth, death, old age and disease. All the residents engage in service to the Lord without selfish personal motivations[83].

They are forests full of auspicious desire trees that fulfill one's desires, and in all seasons they are filled with flowers and fruits because everything there is spiritual and personal[84]. The inhabitants, who have beautiful forms, fly in their airplanes made of emerald and gold. Accompanied by their wives, they constantly and eternally praise the character and activities of the Lord[85]. When the bees praise the glories of the Lord, the pigeon, the cuckoo, the crane, the swan, the parrot, the partridge and the peacock stop their own singing simply to hear the glories of the Lord[86].

After giving the parable of the lantern, quoted above, the Koran gives more details about where it is found: *"this lantern is found in houses which Allah has allowed to be exalted. And in these houses His names are remembered [Koran 24:36]"*. The lantern which represents God is found in exalted houses. Allah, along with His devoted servants, resides in the Lord's abode. These servants are constantly praising His glories. In the Kingdom of God there are activities for the nature of the soul is to be always active. The inhabitants of the Kingdom of God are always engaged in various activities saturated with devotion for the pleasure of the Lord. *"You will see angels surrounding His Throne on all sides, singing His glory and praising their Lord [Koran 39:75]"*.

The Vedic scriptures give elaborate description of God's personal form, qualities, activities and entourage. They recommend worshiping His form and give explicit details of the eternal form of the Lord. The form of Lord is described throughout the Vedic scriptures as having an eternally youthful body. *"The Supreme Lord has a body of eternity, knowledge and bliss. He has no beginning, for He is the beginning of everything. He is the cause of all causes [Bs. 5.1]"*. Such a wonderful description is not the result of some foolish materialistic fertile imagination. These descriptions of the Lord's form are revelations by the Lord to great saintly persons who are unflinchingly surrendered to the Lord's service. This is confirmed in the Koran in the verses quoted above. The foremost [Koran 56:10] will be the nearest to God [Koran 56:12] and enter into His Kingdom. The foremost will be honored [Koran 56:11] in gardens of bliss [Koran 56:12]. If one thoroughly studies the different descriptions of the opulences of the Lord, then one can understand without any doubt the position of Lord and can fix his mind in the worship of God without deviation.

Devotional service

The process of acting for God without being self-interested is called devotional service[87]. It is the best process since no one can live without acting. Everyone acts to maintain his family and their paraphernalia, but no one is working without some self-interest, some personal gratification. The criterion of happiness is to act for God without self-interested intentions. To act for God is the duty of everyone because everyone is a servant of the Supreme Lord.

Actions done for God are not equal to those done for personal sense gratification. As stated in the Koran and the Vedas: "*The faithful who sit at home and receive no hurt is not equal to one who strives in God's cause with his wealth and life. God has granted a higher grade to one who strives with his wealth and life than to one who sits at home [Koran 4:95]". "Work done for the pleasure of Supreme Lord has to be performed; otherwise work causes bondage in this material world. Therefore, O Arjuna, perform your prescribed duties for His satisfaction, and in that way you will always remain free from bondage [Bg.3.9]"*. Activities that are not aimed at the satisfaction of the Lord cause miseries. All activities should be related to the Supreme Lord. No one can be happy without cooperating with the Supreme Lord. Men should offer everything to the service of the Lord because God is the proprietor of the worlds. One has to do his duties without claiming proprietorship. The cashier may count millions of dollars for his employer, but he does not claim a cent for himself. Similarly, one has to realize that nothing in the world belongs to anyone, but that everything belongs to the Supreme Lord. One who avoids serving the Supreme Lord will be degraded. *"Anyone who does not render service and neglects his duty unto the primeval Lord, who is the source of all living entities, will certainly fall down from his constitutional position (SB 11.5.3)."*

The Lord told Arjuna to not give up his prescribed duties. He told him to continue his present engagement and at the same time think of Him. This called devotional service or surrender. *"Therefore, Arjuna, you should always think of Me in the form of Krishna and at the same time carry out your prescribed duty of fighting. With your activities dedicated to Me and your mind and intelligence fixed on Me, you will attain Me without doubt [Bg. 8.7]"*. Some believers made a complaint. They did not want to perform their prescribed duties. They just wanted to pray and give alms to the poor. "*O Lord, why have you made fighting compulsory for us? Why you do not allow us to enjoy life little more? Is it not better to just pray and give little alms to the poor [Koran 4: 77]"? "Is it not better to give drink to the pilgrims and go in pilgrims to the sacred mosque [Koran 9:19]?"* And Allah replied: *"Fighting is prescribed for you even if you dislike it. You may dislike a thing yet it is good for you, and love a thing which is bad for you [Koran 2:216]"*.

Work without self motivation is the beginning of the spiritual path. When selfless work is done with the knowledge that one is a servant of God, one becomes more advanced. When one always thinks of God while carrying out his prescribed duty, one comes to the culmination of action, which is called devotional service. Allah was pleased with the selfless work of the migrant of Mecca[88] and the helpers in Medina[89]. They were the first to believe and they follow Allah's way [Koran 9:100]. "*Allah was kind to the Prophet, the migrant of Mecca, and the helpers in Medina, who followed the prophet in a time of distress. When a section of them was to lose courage, He turned to them in His mercy [Koran 9: 117]"*.

In the beginning of spiritual path, one may have the tendency for mental speculation. One's knowledge about God and His Kingdom may not be perfect. When an individual is further advanced he can understand that in the Kingdom of God there are spiritual activities that constitute devotional service. Realizing this, he becomes attached to God and surrenders to Him. At that time one can understand the Lord's mercy is essential. Also one will understand that the Lord is the cause of everything and that the creation is not independent from Him. He understands that in everything there is a relationship with the Supreme Lord. Thus he thinks of everything in relation to God. With such understanding he fully surrenders to the Supreme Lord. "*When the Lord said to Abraham 'Obey,' he replied, 'I submit to the Lord of all the worlds' [Koran 2:131]*". This same idea is stated in the Vedas. *"Abandon all varieties of religion and just surrender unto Me. I shall deliver you from all sinful reactions. Do not fear [Bg.18.66]"*.

One's level of surrender is tested in difficult time. The surrender soul remembers God and prays to Him to save him from any adverse circumstances. The ignorant forgets God. The most inauspicious time is death. At that time, the material body is abruptly separated from the soul. The hands, legs, ears, eyes and the head are severely separated from the soul as if cut by a cruel butcher. If one is fortunate, at that moment, he will concentrate his thoughts on God. The Lord will help that surrender to soul to die peacefully while remembering Him. At that time, he will give up all varieties of thoughts that have controlled human destiny, and just focus on God. The word 'surrender' has no other meaning than to give up all materialistic thoughts that disturb the mind at the time of death. Surrender means to fully concentrate all thoughts on God. That was the teaching given by Abraham and Jacob to his sons. "*Abraham enjoins upon his sons and so did Jacob, and said, 'O my sons, God has chosen this, as the faith for you. Do not die except in a state of surrender.' [Koran 2:132]*". Jacob also instructed his sons. *"O my sons, God has chosen this, as the faith for you. Do not die except in a state of surrender"*. Lord Krishna has given similar teaching to Arjuna. *"Whoever, at the end of his life, quits his body remembering Me alone at once attains My nature. Of this there is no doubt [Bg. 8.5]". "For one who always remembers Me without deviation, I am easy to obtain, O Arjuna, because of his constant engagement in devotional service [Bg.8.14]"*.

Remembrance of God is neither possible for the self interested fruitive worker who is just interested in how to maintain his body, nor for the argumentative mental speculator. The path of full surrender is difficult to achieve. Material attachment prevents one from giving up his false conception of life. Therefore, all prophets and all believers have tested with the aim to cut off all their material attachment. That they can think of God at the time of death. It is the duty of everyone to focus their life in such a way that they will not forget God at the time of death. One has to always think of God without deviation. One can carry out their prescribed duties in relation to the family, community, nation, humanity and God and at the same time think of God: "*When rites and ceremonies are finished repeat God's names with great concentration [Koran 2:200]"*. The process of thinking of God by the recitation of His names frees one from materialistic mentality. One should constantly remember God. *"Who remembers Allah while standing, sitting and lying on their sides, and who reflect on the creation of the heavens and the earth: Our Lord, You have not created this in vain, all glories to You. Save us from the chastisement of the fire [Koran 3:191]". "Whatever you do, whatever you eat, whatever you offer or give away, and whatever austerities you perform—do that, O Arjuna, as an offering to Me [Bg.9.2]". "Always think of Me, become My devotee, worship Me and offer your homage unto Me. Thus you will come to Me without fail. I promise you this because you are My very dear friend [Bg.18.65]"*. The purpose of the Vedas and the Koran is to teach the process of surrendering to God. Islam means submission to the will of God. Without constant remembrance of the Lord, it is very difficult to surrender to Him. The purpose of all bona fide scriptures is to realize one's eternal relationship with God. As stated in the Vedas, one has to become a servant of God, always think of Him and act for Him.

The Sincere

The path of sense enjoyment is a great stumbling block to spiritual realization. A believer who seeks refuge in the path of renunciation will be elevated to a higher level of spiritual realization. A pretender, who engages in sense enjoyment, will be degraded. One cannot reach a factual understanding of God without renouncing sense enjoyment. The Vedas defines a sincere person as one whose work is done for God without attachment to the result of work. *"On the other hand, if a sincere person tries to control the active senses by the mind and begins work without attachment, he is by far superior [Bg.3:7]."*

The Koran states that a believer, who has faith in God [Koran 2:82] and whose work is righteousness [Koran 2:25], is better than the hypocrite. To be righteous the Koran recommends detachment. *"Unless one gives freely of that which is loved, one cannot attain righteousness [Koran 3:92]"*. A faithful, who is a righteous believer, acts completely for the Lord. Since everything belongs to God, one is called to renounce his material attachments. One has to use all his resources at the service of God, in selfless surrender without material attachment. A sincere person withdraws from worldly attachment and for God's service, he dynamically faces his responsibilities.

Service to God involves using one's possessions, time and energy for His pleasure. To the pretender, material gains, which are destructible, are all in all. As long as a person is illusioned by material gains, he hankers for temporary sensual enjoyment in the form of the heavenly planets. The sincere person is not captivated by such temporary illusory things. They always absorb their activities in the divine thought of God. The ultimate goal of life is God. Material gains are destined to death. In good times, they are like friends, and in bad times, these friends become strangers. The body is also destined to death. When the body collapses and becomes unconscious, the worms and insects will rejoice. They will celebrate a great festival. The body's beauty and strength will not last. The soul, which is eternally young, will awaken by using the body in God's service.

The believer, who uses his body fully in the service of the Lord, has been promised forgiveness [Koran 5:9], reward and protection. He will be given the knowledge of how to come to God. From the depths of darkness he will be lead into light [Koran 2:256]. The Lord uses similitude or parables that are understood only by the believer [Koran 2:254]. The believer has to neither fear, nor grieve [Koran 2:277]. Yet, he is asked to be submissive and obedient. He is commanded to obey God, the messenger and his authority [Koran 4:59]. The believer is commanded to persevere in patience and steadfastness. They have to persevere and help each other [Koran 3:200]. They have to do their duty to the Lord and to seek the means to approach Him. For God's sake they have to not follow their lower desires [Koran 4:135].

To submit to God one has to be free from hate and have equal vision towards all living beings. *"To act equitably is nearer to piety and is pleasing to Allah [Koran 5:8]". "O you who believe, be upright for Allah, bearers of witness with justice, and let not hatred of a people incite you not to act equitably; act equitably, that is nearer to piety, and be careful of Allah[Koran 5:8]".* A believer is urged to fear the dualities of hate and desire. Under these dualities, one loses the power to act equitably. Due to desire and hate one becomes bewildered. One dwells in the dualities of honor and dishonor, friend and enemy, poor and rich and pleasure and pain. Human beings are meant to realize peace, prosperity and brotherhood in a cooperative spirit as members of the Lord's spiritual community.

Spiritual Harmony

In order to appreciate others faith better, one has to reach a consistent understanding of the Supreme Lord and the subordinate relationship that all living beings have with Him. All opposing difficulties can be dispelled by being in absolute harmony with the Lord who is the well wisher of all living beings. The byproduct of such an understanding is tolerance which is based on accepting the absolute position of God, rather than denying Him.

Tolerance is based on the understanding that God is pleased by devotional service and not materially motivated rituals. If faith in the Lord is weak due to impure consciousness, intolerance arises. In pure faith, one sees God, his religion, his teachings, his prophets and his servant as one. If God is one, His teachings are also one. Since God is one, His order must be one. Since all the prophets and sages, from time immemorial, had served God, with different means, they should be regarded with a favorable disposition in their original freedom of choice and behavior in glorifying the almighty God. Out of intolerance, different foolish religious leaders consider their God to be different from the God of others, but that is not possible. God, who has different names, is the same. Allah, Jehovah, Krishna etc. should be glorified with great vigor. No one can claim that only Jehovah's name is worthy of belief. One should first strengthen his faith.

Purification of consciousness through devotional service to God strengthens this faith. Material desire pollutes one's consciousness. For the purpose of true religious tolerance, all scriptures recommend the glorification of the sacred Names of God. True glorification of God results in clear understanding of the nature of God. Once God is understood, harmony and love among men arise. Unhealthy habits and attitudes automatically disappear. Religion that consists only of external rituals or even of getting everyone to accept the same exact scripture or the same form and name of God will not bring universal harmony. This harmony emerges in purified consciousness that is absorbed in fulfilling the will of the Lord. As comprehension of the Supreme Lord arises, tolerance and respect of others scriptures through understanding arises in man. One who blasphemes other scriptures and their followers that glorify the Lord, displease the Lord. One has not to criticize others' methods of religion. Instead of criticizing such systems, one has to encourage the followers to stick to their principles so that they gradually can develop a pure consciousness. By simply criticizing them, one creates great disturbances in the society. People's mind becomes very agitated. One should learn to tolerate and stop all agitation.

The aim of the Vedic system and the Koran is to elevate the seeker of God from a state of polluted consciousness to a state of pure consciousness. In polluted consciousness, one is illusioned by lust, hate and greed. An illusioned man cannot understand what is what. Instead of advancing in spiritual revelation, one becomes more and more degraded. In polluted consciousness, one does not possess perfect wisdom nor does he know what real enjoyment is. Bewildered by his shadow belief, one strives for pleasure that results in suffering. Only in pure consciousness one is able to see things as they are for one's true benefit. For proper tolerance and mutual understanding, the Koran and the Vedas recommends the process for the true evolution of consciousness. Śrī Chaitanya Mahāprabhu, five hundred years ago in his interfaith dialogue with that great saintly Muslim, has given the process for the true evolution of consciousness. Evolution towards perfection begins when there is a transition from identification with matter to spirit. One has not to see himself separate from God. Rather one has to develop a spiritual relationship with God.

According to the Koran and the Vedic scriptures, the kingdom of God is the supreme residential place where the Lord resides along with His eternal servants. The Koran and Vedic literatures both reveal the Lord in His all pervading effulgence aspect, His expansions within all living beings and the full revelation of Him in His eternal Kingdom. The faithful accepts these statements, modeling his life and acting upon them. In the Kingdom of God there is complete harmony between its residents and the Supreme Lord. *"You will see angels surrounding His Throne on all sides, singing His glory and praising their Lord [Koran 39:75]"*. In the Kingdom of God the Lord is perfect and its inhabitants are perfectly engaged in His service. There is no fear there because of the united interests of the Lord and its residents. There are no politics of divide and rule caused by separate interest in the Kingdom of God.

A servant of the Lord no longer wastes valuable time in speculating. He accepts the statements as revealed in the Holy Scriptures. He knows perfectly well that everything belongs to the Lord. Therefore, he engages everything in His service and does not create perplexities by falsely trying to be the master over the creation of the Lord. He is so faithful that he engages himself, as well as everything else, in the transcendental service of the Lord since everything is coming from Him. In everything, the servant sees the Lord, and he sees everything and everyone in relation to the Lord. Such peace, harmony and truth lies only in understanding the essence of the Lord's message.

Bibliography

• Major Themes in the Koran Bibliotheca Islamica Rahman, Fazlur1989

• The History of the Koranic Text from Revelation to Compilation, UK Islamic Academy: Leicester. Al-Azami, M. M 2003

• The Monotheists: Jews, Christians, and Muslims in Conflict and Competition Princeton University Press. Peters, Francis E. (2003).

• Islam: Religion, History, and Civilization. Harper San Francisco Nasr, Seyyed Hossein Nasr (2003).

• An Introduction to Islamic Cosmological Doctrines: Conceptions of Nature. SUNY Press Nasr, Seyyed Hossein Nasr (1993b).

• What Everyone Needs to Know about Islam. Oxford University Press Esposito, John (2002)

• Bhagavad-gita As it Is BBT, Los Angeles A.C. Bhaktivedanta Swami Prabhupada

• Islam: A Thousand Years of Faith and Power. New Haven: Yale University Press. 2002.

• Approaching the Qur'an (White Cloud Press, 1999) Michael Sells,

• A student's approach to world religions: Islam, Hodder & Stoughton Watton, Victor, (1993).

• Nectar of Devotion BBT, Los Angeles A.C. Bhaktivedanta Swami Prabhupada

• Introduction to Islam, M. Cherif Bassiouni Publisher:Rand Mcnally, 1989

• Islam: The way of submission, Aquarian Press Solomon Nigosian, 150

• Srimad Bhagavatam canto 1 to 12 BBT, Los Angeles A.C. Bhaktivedanta Swami Prabhupada

• The Historical Jesus: The Life of a Mediterranean Jewish Peasant. New York: Harper San Francisco, 1993.

• The Logia of Yeshua: The sayings of Jesus. Washington, DC: Counterpoint, 1996. Davenport, Guy; and Urrutia, Benjamin(trans.)

• Nectar of Instruction BBT, Los Angeles A.C. Bhaktivedanta Swami Prabhupada

• The Lost Christianities: The Battles for Scripture and the Faiths We Never Knew. New York: Oxford University Press, 2003. Ehrman, Bart.

• The Higher Taste BBT, Los Angeles A.C. Bhaktivedanta Swami Prabhupada

• Jesus of Nazareth, King of the Jews: A Jewish Life and the Emergence of Christianity. New York: Vintage, 2000. Fredriksen, Paula.

• Jesus and Judaism Minneapolis: Fortress Press, 1987 Sanders, E.P:

•Caitanya-caritamrta BBT, Los Angeles A.C. Bhaktivedanta Swami Prabhupada

• Brahma Samhita BBT, Los Angeles Bhaktisidhanta Swami Prabhupada

• Jesus in his Jewish Context Minneapolis: Augsburg Fortress, 2003 Vermes, Geza.

• Living Judaism: The Complete Guide to Jewish Belief, Tradition and Practice Wayne Dosick.

• A History of the Jews Paul Johnson, HarperCollins, 1988
• Science of Self-Realization BBT, Los Angeles A.C. Bhaktivedanta Swami Prabhupada
• The Jews of Islam Princeton: Princeton University Press. Lewis, Bernard (1984).
• Krsna Book BBT, Los Angeles A.C. Bhaktivedanta Swami Prabhupada
• Semites and Anti-Semites: An Inquiry into Conflict and Prejudice. W. W. Norton & Co. Lewis, Bernard (1999).
• The Koran Interpreted: A Translation (1st Ed.). Touchstone Arberry, A. J. (1996)
• Noble Quran (1st Ed.). Dar-us-Salam Publications: Khan, Muhammad Muhsin; Al-Hilali Khan, Muhammad Taqi-ud-Din (1999).
• Islam in History: Ideas, People, and Events in the Middle East. Open Court. Lewis, Bernard (1993).
• Islam and the West. Oxford University Press Lewis, Bernard (1994)
• Cultures in Conflict: Christians, Muslims, and Jews in the Age of Discovery: Oxford University Press. Lewis, Bernard (1996).
• The Sealed Nectar: Biography of the Prophet: Dar-us Salam Publications. Mubarkpuri, Saifur-Rahman (2002).
• History of Islam. Dar-us-Salam Publications: Najeebabadi, Akbar Shah (2001).
• Islam: Its History, Teaching, and Practices (New Edition ed.). Indiana University Press. Nigosian, S. A. (2004).
• Bhakti Rasamrta Sindhu Srila Rupa Goswami (BBT, Los Angeles)
• Islam (2nd ed.). University of Chicago Press. Rahman, Fazlur (1979)
• Shri Ishopanisad BBT, Los Angeles A.C. Bhaktivedanta Swami Prabhupada
• Foundations of Islam: The Making of a World Faith. Peter Owen Publishers: Walker, Benjamin (1998).
• Islam Today: A Short Introduction to the Muslim World (2.00 Ed.). I. B. Tauris Ahmed, Akbar (1999).
• Muhammad: A Prophet for our Time. HarperCollins Armstrong, Karen (2006).
• Islam: The Straight Path (3rd Ed.). Oxford University Press: Esposito, John (1998).
• Oxford History of Islam Oxford University Press: Esposito, John (2000b).
• Unholy War: Terror in the Name of Islam. Oxford University Press: Esposito, John (2002a).
• Path of Perfection BBT, Los Angeles A.C. Bhaktivedanta Swami Prabhupada
• What Everyone Needs to Know about Islam. Oxford University Press: Esposito, John (2002b).
• Islam: Beliefs and Observances (5th Ed.). Barron's Educational Series: Farah, Caesar (1994).
• Islam: Beliefs and Observances (7th Ed.). Barron's Educational Series: Farah, Caesar (2003).
• Jihad: The Origin of Holy War in Islam. Oxford University Press: Firestone, Reuven (1999).

- Tolerance and Coercion in Islam: Interfaith Relations in the Muslim Tradition. Cambridge University Press: Friedmann, Yohanan (2003).
- Dynamics of Islam: An Exposition. Trafford Publishing: Hedayetullah, Muhammad (2006).
- Cambridge History of Islam, Vol.1 Cambridge University Press: Holt, P. M.; Bernard Lewis (1977a).
- Cambridge History of Islam, Vol.2 Cambridge University Press: Holt, P. M.; Ann K. S. Lambton, Bernard Lewis (1977b).
- A History of the Arab Peoples Belknap Press; Revised edition Hourani, Albert; Ruthven, Malise (2003)
- The Crisis of Islam: Holy War and Unholy Terror Random House, Inc., New York Lewis, Bernard (2004).
- The Succession to Muhammad: A Study of the Early Caliphate Cambridge University Press Madelung, Wilferd (1996).
- Islam: A Guide for Jews and Christians. Princeton University Press Peters, F. E. (2003).
- Jihad in Medieval and Modern Islam Brill Academic Publishers Peters, Rudolph (1977)
- Muslims: Their Religious Beliefs and Practices (2nd Ed.). Routledge Rippin, Andrew (2001)
- Fundamentalism: The Search for Meaning. Oxford University Press Ruthven, Malise (2005)
- The Islamic Understanding of Death and Resurrection Oxford University Press Smith, Jane I. (2006)
- Islam: the Basics. Routledge (UK) Turner, Colin (2006)
- Muhammad: Prophet and Statesman (New Ed.). Oxford University Press Watt, W. Montgomery (1974)
- Vedanta Sutra Commentary by Baladeva Vidyabushana (Krishna Institute, USA)

References

1 Shrī Chaitanya Mahāprabhu, (1486-1534): He appeared in Navadvīpa, West Bengal, India and inaugurated the congregational chanting of the holy names of the Lord to teach pure love of God.

2 Vaiṣhṇavism: the science of devotional service to Viṣṇu, or Krishna

3 Bible Ezra 1:1-4, 2 Chron 36:22-23; Dan. 9:1-2

4 Josephus, *War of the Jews* II.8.11, II.13.7, II.14.4, II.14.5

5 Dhhaime, Jean, Blasi, Anthony J, Turcotte, Paul Andri (2000):
Handbook of early Christianity: Social science Approaches. Walnut, Caliph, Alta Mira Press p.434

6 Wylen (1995). Pg 190. Berard (2006). Pp 112-113. Wright (1992). Pp 164-165

7 This condemnation included many groups, of which the Christians were but one. This did not necessarily mean excommunication.

8 According to the Book of Acts, and according to the Catholic Encyclopedia: Martin Buber, "The Two Foci of the Jewish Soul," cited in The Writings of Martin Buber, Will Herberg (editor), New York: Meridian Books, 1956, p. 276.

9 H.H. Ben-Sasson, *A History of the Jewish People*, Harvard University Press, 1976,

10 Bokenkotter, *A Concise History of the Catholic Church* (2004), p. 18, quote: "The story of how this tiny community of believers spread to many cities of the Roman Empire within less than a century is indeed a remarkable chapter in the history of humanity."

11 Bargil Pixner, *The Church of the Apostles found on Mount Zion*, Biblical Archaeology Review 16.3 May/June 1990

12 "Roman Empire", Microsoft Encarta Online Encyclopedia 2008

13 [Koran 2.3-4]

14 [Koran 42.7]

15 Seyyed Hossein Nasr (April., 2003):The Heart of Islam, Enduring Values for Humanity, pp 3, 39, 85, 27–272

16 [Koran 2.177]

17 [Koran 2.177]

18 [Koran 2.184]

19 Farah (1994), pp.145–147; Goldschmidt (2005) p.48. in Encyclopedia Britannica Online

20 Chaitanya-charitāmṛta is translated as "the character of the living force in immortality". It is the title of the authorized biography of Shri Chaitanya Mahāprabhu written in the late sixteenth century. It was compiled by Śrīla Kṛṣṇadāsa Kavirāja Gosvāmī. Written in Bengali, with many Sanskrit verses as well. It is regarded as the most authoritative book on Lord Chaitanya's life and teachings; Written by Śrīla Kṛṣṇadāsa Kavirāja Gosvāmī, this biography of Shri Chaitanya Mahāprabhu is the single most important text of Gauḍīya Vaiṣṇava philosophy. Chaitanya-caritāmṛta is the postgraduate study of spiritual

knowledge, and so is not intended for the novice. Ideally, one begins with Bhagavad-gītā and advances through Śrīmad-Bhāgavatam to the Śrī Chaitanya-caritāmṛta. Although all these great scriptures are on the same absolute level, for the sake of comparative study Śrī Chaitanya-caritāmṛta is considered to be on the highest platform.

21 A.C. Bhaktivedanta Swami Prabhupada Chaitanya-charitamrta (BBT, Los Angeles) [CC Madhya 18.186]

22 A.C. Bhaktivedanta Swami Prabhupada Chaitanya-charitamrta (BBT, Los Angeles) [CC Madhya 18.188]

23 A.C. Bhaktivedanta Swami Prabhupada Chaitanya-charitamrta (BBT, Los Angeles) [CC Madhya 18.193]

24 [Koran 12:2] Solomon Nigosian, Islam: The Way Of Submission

25 Cherif Bassiouni M. Introduction to Islam

26 Cherif Bassiouni M. Introduction to Islam

27 Cherif Bassiouni M. Introduction to Islam

28 Solomon Nigosian, Islam: The Way Of Submission

29 Cherif Bassiouni M. Introduction to Islam

30 Solomon Nigosian, Islam: The Way Of Submission

31 Madhvacarya is one of the principal teachers of Vedic philosophy commenting on the Vedānta-sūtra (2.1.6), quotes the Bhaviṣya Purāṇa as follows: ṛg-yajuḥ-sāmārtharvāś ca / bhāratam pañcarātrakam / mūla-rāmāyaṇaṁ caiva / veda ity eva śabditaḥ / purāṇāni ca yānīha / vaiṣṇavāni vido viduḥ : «The Ṛg Veda, Yajur Veda, Sāma Veda, Atharva Veda, Mahābhārata, which includes the Bhagavad-gītā, Pañcarātra, and the original Rāmāyaṇa are all considered Vedic literature . . . The Vaiṣṇava supplements, the Purāṇas, are also Vedic literature». We may also include corollary literatures like the Saṁhitās, as well as the commentaries of the great teachers in disciplic succession who have guided the course of Vedic thought for centuries.

32 Vedānta-sūtra: Athāto brahma jijñāsā (1.1.1).

33 Mental speculator: Jñānī—one who is engaged in the cultivation of knowledge especially by philosophical speculation. This Sanskrit term is related in both form and meaning to the English word knows via the Greek word gnsis. In Vedic terminology, there is jñāna and vijñāna. Jñāna refers to the knowledge of the self as not the body, whereas vijñāna refers to knowledge of the self in relationship to the Supreme Self.

34 Quoted in Vedānta-sūtra (1.3.2): tarati śokam ātma-vit: "One who knows the Supreme crosses beyond grief." [Chāndogya Upaniṣad 7.1.3]

35 Mystic: From the Greek mystes, one initiated into the mysteries or secrets of higher knowledge. Mysticism is a process that is performed for the purpose of developing subtle material powers.

36 Vedānta-sūtra: ānandamayo ‹bhyāsāt: "The Supreme Lord is by nature full of joy." [Vedanta-sutra 1.1.12]

37 A.C. Bhaktivedanta Swami Prabhupada Bhagavad gita as it is (BBT, Los Angeles) brahma-bhūtaḥ prasannātmā / na śocati na kāṅkṣati / samaḥ sarveṣu bhūteṣu / mad-bhaktiṁ labhate parām: "One who is thus transcendentally situated at once realizes the Supreme

Brahman and becomes fully joyful. He never laments or desires to have anything. He is equally disposed toward every living entity. In that state he attains pure devotional service unto Me [Bg. 18:54]."

38 Tattva-Sandarbha, annucheda 17 By Śrīla Jīva Gosvāmī ebook

39 A.C. Bhaktivedanta Swami Prabhupada Chaitanya-charitamrta (BBT, Los Angeles) [Cc. Madhya 25.145]

40 The victory of Badr was decisive for it was the first time that the Koresh government was defeated along with his nobles by a band of amateur people. With this victory a new power had arisen in Arabia. The authority of the apostle was strengthened in the region. The local Arab tribes began to convert and ally themselves with the Muslims and the expansion of Islam began. At that time, Arabia was populated by a number of Arabic speaking peoples. Some were Bedouin; pastoral nomads organized in tribes; and other were doing agriculture. The majority of Arabs were adherents of numerous polytheistic religions. There were also tribes that followed Judaism, Christianity, Nestorians' and Zoroastrianism.

In 622, an open act of violence was committed by the Koresh tribesmen against the Muslims. The apostle and many of his followers fled to the neighboring city of Medina. This migration is called the Hijra and marked the beginning of Muhammad's reign as both a political as well as a religious leader.

A caravan, commanded by Abu Sufyan and guarded by thirty to forty men, was travelling from Syria back to Mecca. The caravan was funded with the money of the Muslims that have fled from Mecca to the city of Medina. The Koresh sold all their belongings and used the money to fund this caravan. The apostle gathered the first largest Muslims army of three hundred men. The apostle commanded the army himself and brought many of his top commandeers including Hamzah, Abu Bakr, Omar, and Ali. As the caravan approached Medina, Abu Sufyan began hearing from travelers and riders about Muhammad's planned ambush. He sent a messenger to Mecca to get reinforcements from the Koresh. Alarmed, the Koresh assembled an army of one thousand men to rescue the caravan. When news reached the Muslim army about the departure of the army of Mecca, the apostle called a council of war, since there was still time to retreat and because many of the fighters were recent converts, called Ansar or helpers.

The army of Mecca expected an easy victory against the Muslims who were less in number. The Koresh broke camp and marched into the valley of Badr and both armies engaged in combat. The force of the Muslim attack is described in several Koranic verses, which refer that thousands of angels descending from Heaven at Badr to slaughter the Koresh.

There are several narration from the tradition where the apostle discusses with the Angel Gabriel the role he played in the battle. The people of Mecca quickly broke and ran away from the battlefield. The battle lasted for few hours only and was over by the early afternoon.

The Meccan losses were seventy dead and seventy captured. Muslim losses were fourteen killed.

41 Sahih Bukhari Vol 1, Book 4. Ablutions Hadith 241

42 Koresh was the dominant tribe of Mecca upon the appearance of the religion of Islam. It was the tribe to which Muhammad belonged, as well as the tribe that led the initial opposition to his message.

43 [Koran 8:11]

44 Mahābhārata is an ancient, Sanskrit, epic history of India. It was composed by Kṛṣṇa Dvaipāyana Vyāsadeva in 100,000 verses. The essence of all Vedic philosophy, the Bhagavad-gītā, is a part of this great work. Mahabhārata is a history of the earth from its creation to the great Kurukṣetra war fought between the Kuru and Pāṇḍava factions of the Kaurava dynasty, which took place about five thousand years ago. The battle was waged to determine who would be the emperor of the world: the saintly Yudhiṣthira, a Vaiṣṇava king, or the evil-minded Duryodhana, the son of Dhrtarastra.

45 The battle of Kurukṣetra is a battle between the Kurus and the Pāṇḍavas, which took place five thousand years ago and before which Lord Kṛṣṇa spoke Bhagavad-gītā to Arjuna.

46 Pāṇḍu is a great king of the Kuru dynasty, and the father of the Pāṇḍavas, Yudhisthira, Bhima, Arjuna, Nakula and Sahadeva; the heroes of the Mahābhārata. He had two wives, Kuntī and Mādrī. He was a younger brother of Dhṛtarāṣṭra. He died early, leaving his five young sons under the care of his blind brother Dhṛtarāṣṭra.

47 Dhṛtarāṣṭra is the father of the Kauravas. He was born of the union of the great sage Vyāsadeva and Ambikā. He was born blind because Ambikā closed her eyes during conception, out of fear of the sage. He was reputed to have the strength of ten thousand elephants. The attempt to usurp the Pāṇḍavas' kingdom for the sake of his own sons resulted in the Kurukṣetra war. Bhagavad-gītā was related to Dhṛtarāṣṭra by his secretary as it was being spoken on the Battlefield of Kurukṣetra.

48 The five Pāṇḍavas are Arjuna, Maharaja Yudhistira, Bhima, Nakula and Sahadeva.

49 A.C. Bhaktivedanta Swami Prabhupada Bhagavad gita As it is (BBT, Los Angeles) [Bg.2.4-6]

50 A.C. Bhaktivedanta Swami Prabhupada Bhagavad gita As it is (BBT, Los Angeles) [Bg.2.7-8]

51 A.C. Bhaktivedanta Swami Prabhupada Bhagavad gita As it is (BBT, Los Angeles) [Bg.1.29-30]

52 A.C. Bhaktivedanta Swami Prabhupada Bhagavad gita As it is

(BBT, Los Angeles) [Bg. 2.2]

53 According to the historian William Henry Chamberlin

54 According to the historian William Henry Chamberlin

55 Abu Bakr, 573 CE–23 August 634 was one of the first to convert to Islam. He was a senior companion of Muhammad. Upon Muhammad's death he became the first Muslim ruler 632–634 CE. His caliphate lasted two years and three months. He fought against the Arab tribes to establish an Islamic rule over all of Arabia. He also conquered the lands of Syria and Iraq.

56 Omar, 586-590 CE, was a companion of Muhammad. He succeeded Abu Bakr (632–634) as the second Caliph. Under him the Islamic empire expanded at an unprecedented rate

annexing the whole Persian Empire and more than two thirds of the Eastern Roman Empire.

57 Othman, 579-656 CE was one of the companions of Muhammad. He played a major role in early Islamic history, most notably as the third Caliph.

58 Ali was the cousin and son-in-law of Muhammad, who ruled over the Islamic Caliphate from 656 to 661. Ali was appointed caliph after the assassination of the third caliph. He encountered defiance and civil war during his reign. In 661, Ali was attacked while praying in the mosque of Kufa. Few days later, he died.

59 pravṛttir eṣā bhūtānāṁ nivṛttis tu mahā-phalā

60 [Koran 2:12]

61 [Koran 2:14]

62 [Koran 7:101]

63 [Koran 7:132]

64 [Koran 2:41]

65 [Koran 2:28]

66 The ‘Ad occupied what is now eastern Yemen and western Oman, running from the Arabian Sea up into the Dhofar Mountains and to the edge of the Rab al-Khali.

67 A.C. Bhaktivedanta Swami Prabhupada Bhagavad gita As it is (BBT, Los Angeles) (Bg7.20-23)

68 Agni: the demigod who controls fire.

69 A.C. Bhaktivedanta Swami Prabhupada Śrīmad-Bhāgavatam (BBT, Los Angeles) [SB 2.3.2-7], [SB 2.3.9]

70 Ibn Abbas narrated: “After the death of some righteous men, Satan inspired their people to erect statues in the places where they used to sit. At first, these statues were not worshiped. Later, the coming generations started to worship them as their idols.”

Ibn Jarir narrated: “There were some righteous people who lived between the period of Adam and Noah. After their death, their friends and followers said: “If we make statues of them, it will be more pleasing to us in our worship and will remind us of them.” So they built statues of them, and after they had died and others came after them, Satan crept into their minds saying, “Your forefathers used to worship them for getting rain”. So they worshipped them.

Ibn Abi Hatim related this story: “Waddan was a righteous man who was loved by his people. When he died, they withdrew to his grave in the land of Babylonia and were overwhelmed by sadness. When Satan saw their sorrow caused by his death, he disguised himself in the form of a man saying: ‘I have seen your sorrow because of this man’s death. Can I make a statue like him which could be put in your meeting place to make you remember him?’ They said: ‘Yes.’ So he made the statue like him. They put it in their meeting place in order to be reminded of him. When Satan saw their interest in remembering him, he said: ‘Can I build a statue of him in the home of each one of you so that he would be in everyone’s house and you could remember him?’ They agreed. Their children learned about and saw what they were doing. They also learned about their remembrance of him instead of God. So the first to be worshipped instead of God was Waddan, the idol which they named thus.”

71 Ibn Abbas narrated that the Prophet Muhammad said: "The period between Adam and Noah was ten centuries." (Sahih Bukhari), Noah was born 1056 years after Adam's creation or after he left the Garden of Eden.

72 Paramātmā is the Supersoul, the localized aspect of the Supreme Lord that is residing in the heart of each embodied living entity and pervading over everything.

73 "We created man from a product of wet earth [Koran 23:12]".

74 prajñayā śarīraṁ samāruhya

75 Smṛti-śāstra

76 Krishna Book BBT, Los Angeles A.C. Bhaktivedanta Swami Prabhupada chapter 15 The Killing of Dhenukāsura

77 M. R. Bawa Muhaiyaddeen, Asma' ul-Husna: The 99 Beautiful Names of Allah, 1979, p. 182

78 Diet and Stress in Vascular Disease, Journal of the American Medical Association, June 3, 1961, p. 806.

79 Quoted from Cancer and Other Diseases from Meat Consumption, Blanche Leonardo, Ph.D., 1979, p. 12

80 A.C. Bhaktivedanta Swami Prabhupada Śrīmad-Bhāgavatam (BBT, Los Angeles) [SB 7.13.25] purport

81 "One should serve the Supreme Lord favorably without desire for material profit or gain through motivated activities of philosophical speculation. That is called pure devotional service [Bhaktirasāmṛta-sindhu 1.1.11]."

82 A.C. Bhaktivedanta Swami Prabhupada Śrīmad-Bhāgavatam (BBT, Los Angeles) [SB 3.15.17]

83 A.C. Bhaktivedanta Swami Prabhupada Śrīmad-Bhāgavatam (BBT, Los Angeles) [SB 3.15.18]

84 Bhaktisiddānta Sarasvatī Ṭhākura, Śrī Brahma-saṁhitā(BBT, Los Angeles) "I worship Govinda, the primeval Lord, who is endowed with great power. The glowing effulgence of His transcendental form is the impersonal effulgence, which is absolute, complete and unlimited [Bs. 5.40]".

85 A.C. Bhaktivedanta Swami Prabhupada Śrīmad-Bhāgavatam (BBT, Los Angeles) [SB 3.15.13]

86 A.C. Bhaktivedanta Swami Prabhupada Śrīmad-Bhāgavatam (BBT, Los Angeles) [SB 3.15.14]

87 A.C. Bhaktivedanta Swami Prabhupada Śrīmad-Bhāgavatam (BBT, Los Angeles) [SB 3.15.16]

88 The Arabic name for those who emigrated from Mecca to Medina is Muhajir

89 The citizens of Medina are called the helpers, Ansar. When Muhammad was persecuted by the chief leader of Mecca, the citizens of Medina invited to him to reside with them in Medina.

Abbreviations used throughout this book:

Bg. Bhagavad-gītā
Brs. Bhakti-rasāmṛta-sindhu
CC. Caitanya-caritāmṛta
Iso. Śrī Īśopaniṣad
SB. Śrīmad-Bhāgavatam
Bs. Brahma-saṁhitā